SERVANTS IN CHARGE

Servants in Charge

A Training Manual for Elders and Deacons

.

Keith M. Bailey

WingSpread Publishers
Chicago, Illinois

WingSpread Publishers
Chicago, Illinois

www.moodypublishers.com

An imprint of Moody Publishers

Servants in Charge
ISBN: 978-1-60066-104-4
LOC Catalog Card Number: 2006924729
© 1979 by Moody Bible Institute

Previously published by Christian Publications, Inc.
First Christian Publications edition 1979
First WingSpread Publishers edition 2006

CONTENTS

Preface

> *"Be on guard! Be alert! You do not know when that time will come. It's like a man going away: He leaves his house in charge of his servants, each with his assigned task, and tells the one at the door to keep watch. So you also must keep watch because you do not know when the owner of the house will come back—whether in the evening, or at midnight, or when the rooster crows, or at dawn. If he comes suddenly don't let him find you sleeping. What I say to you, I say to everyone: Watch!" (Mark 13:33-37 - NIV)*
>
> *Jesus said on another occasion, ". . . but whoever wishes to become great among you shall be your servant." (Matt. 20:26)*

This passage is taken from the Olivet discourse which was Jesus' longest sermon about His second coming. After giving the signs of His return and the great apocalyptic events of the end time, Jesus, in simple language, spoke about His church during this age. The care of the house was His primary concern. Since Christ contemplated being absent from the church for an unknown period of time He addressed Himself to the problem of the care and oversight of the house during that period. Christ valued His house and longed to find it watchful and ready at His return.

Jesus placed His servants in charge of the house of God during His absence. The kinds of servants that would supervise His house, the church, are not defined in this passage, but the Holy Spirit subsequently taught the apostles the refinements of that divinely commissioned servanthood. The servants had differing responsibilities in the house. Ephesians 4:11 lists those servants whose responsibility is to train and edify all the other

7

servants of the house of God. The officers in charge were later identified as the elders and deacons. Among the elders were to be pastor-elders and lay-elders.

Churchmen should learn from Scripture the kinds of servants in Christ's house and their respective functions, and what it means for them to be in charge.

Have you ever been in an office or a place of business when someone entered the door and asked the question, "Who is in charge here?" Perhaps it is not fanciful thinking to believe that, as they enter the church, many new Christians are asking, "Who is in charge here?" The answer was given by Jesus in a beautiful parable about His second coming. Jesus put His servants in charge until He personally returns to His house.

No human plan for the oversight of the house of God can improve upon the plan Christ Himself revealed. Those in charge of Christ's house are not so much known for their position as for their attitude—they are servants.

1

Local Church Leadership

The Book of Exodus narrates the formation of God's ancient covenant people, Israel. God called a leader and prepared him to assume the oversight of Israel before He brought the nation out of Egypt. Moses proved to be a bold and competent leader.

As the people of God progressed in their wilderness journey toward the land of promise, Moses found himself confronted with an overwhelming leadership work load. The pressure of ministering daily from early morning till late in the day was draining his strength and frustrating the people. It apparently had not occurred to Moses that a larger leadership corps was needed so that he could delegate some responsibilities to others. When this situation was reaching a crisis level, Moses was honored by a visit from his father-in-law Jethro. Though Jethro was a humble shepherd from the back country he was a man of keen insight. After observing his son-in-law's strenuous work schedule for some days Jethro made a suggestion to Moses as to how he might free himself from the frustrations of overwork.

> And Moses' father-in-law said to him, "The thing that you are doing is not good.
>
> "You will surely wear out, both yourself and these people who are with you, for the task is too heavy for you; you cannot do it alone.
>
> "Now listen to me: I shall give you counsel, and God be with you. You be the people's representative before God, and you bring the disputes to God,
>
> "then teach them the statutes and the laws, and make known to them the way in which they are to walk, and the work they are to do.
>
> "Furthermore, you shall select out of all the people able

9

men who fear God, men of truth, those who hate dishonest gain; and you shall place these over them, as leaders of thousands, of hundreds, of fifties and of tens.

"And let them judge the people at all times; and let it be that every major dispute they will bring to you, but every minor dispute they themselves will judge. So it will be easier for you, and they will bear the burden with you.

"If you do this thing and God so commands you, then you will be able to endure; and all these people also will go to their place in peace."

So Moses listened to his father-in-law, and did all that he had said.

And Moses chose able men out of all Israel, and made them heads over the people, leaders of thousands, of hundreds, of fifties and of tens.

And they judged the people at all times; the difficult dispute they would bring to Moses, but every minor dispute they themselves would judge. (Ex. 18:17-26)

The wise counsel of that old layman probably saved the ministry of Moses. The principles of leadership pointed out by Jethro still need to be applied in the household of faith. The need for multiple leaders is as important in the New Testament church as it was in Israel. The pastor who never discovers the blessing of fellow-leaders will face frustration and failure throughout his ministry. Some Bible teachers believe that Moses forfeited much of his leadership authority and blessing when he listened to Jethro's advice. But the Bible does not say that. Not one word of rebuke or check came to Moses from the Lord. Moses was a stronger leader in subsequent days. He did not have to abdicate his leadership to form a system of supportive leaders to meet the growing needs of the people.

The pastor of a church needs the assistance and support of well-trained, godly elders and deacons. In the congregation of Israel, Jehovah not only selected leadership, but He also revealed structures of organization. He created offices. The Holy Spirit directed the early Christian leaders in a similar pattern by establishing offices and structures designed to promote the growth of the church.

The plea for an unstructured church life is based on misunderstanding of the divine plan for church government. The New Testament at no point advocates an unstructured church. It teaches that the worship and activity of the church is to be Spirit-structured. The structures of the spiritually alive church are vital. The quality of leadership determines to some extent the workableness of organizational structures. A new system will not replace Spirit-filled, committed leadership.

The necessity of leadership is a fundamental principle in both the Old Testament and the New Testament. God has always had leaders for His household. Israel had Abraham, Moses, and David. The church of the New Testament had Peter, James, John, and Paul. Every crisis in the history of the redemption community has been resolved by God-given leadership. God's method is a man commissioned to lead.

The health and growth of the church are closely related to its leadership. Right structures, workable organization, and competent leadership are part of the Spirit's order for Christ's church on earth.

Christ considered leadership so important that He devoted a major part of His ministry to training the twelve apostles. Christ knew they would have the leadership responsibility thrust upon them when He ascended to the Father.

God the Father appointed Jesus Christ as Head over all things to the church (Eph. 1:22). As the Redeemer of the church and as Head of the church Christ provided for human leadership in the community of faith. Richard L. Dresselhaus says,

> "Jesus did not leave His church without leadership. Arising out of the New Testament narrative is a structure that served the church well in the first century. Under properly appointed leaders, the church moved forward in unity and strength."[1]

In reality the church is dependent on competent leadership and sound organization. The New Testament makes that plain. To assume that a truly Spirit-directed church has no structure and no definable leadership is to be utterly deceived.

The realities of human society demonstrate that men from the most primitive to the most complex societies must find and observe workable structures of organization if they are to survive. Modern sociology has learned much about the principles of leadership and structure in the total societal realm.

It is inherent in the church as a society of people that it should have both leadership and organizational structure. Because of the church's origin and spiritual dimension it should have distinct structures to achieve its purpose. The sociology of religion may give interesting insight into the church's leadership and government, but it is the Bible which provides the ultimate directive for the church.

The Character of Leadership

The attitude of leadership is important. Christ in His teachings and practice provides the ideal model for leadership at any level. Jesus' most frequent designation for His leader was that of servant. Christ revealed to His disciples a heavenly perception of leadership. This was difficult for the disciples to understand since they had an earthly view of leadership. On more than one occasion they discussed among themselves the possibilities of leadership in Christ's kingdom. Each time Christ rebuked them for assuming the viewpoint of the world in determining leaders.

James and John, the sons of Zebedee, came to Jesus seeking the position on the right hand and the left hand of His throne in the Kingdom.

> *And calling them to Himself, Jesus said to them, "You know that those who are recognized as rulers of the Gentiles lord it over them; and their great men exercise authority over them.*
> *"But it is not so among you, but whoever wishes to become great among you shall be your servant;*
> *"And whoever wishes to be first among you shall be slave of all.*
> *"For even the Son of Man did not come to be served, but to serve, and to give His life a ransom for many." (Mark 10:42-45)*

At the Last Supper there was a dispute among the disciples about the privilege of leadership they would enjoy. With tenderness Jesus corrected their carnal viewpoint by pointing out His own example.

> *"For who is greater, the one who reclines at table, or the one who serves? Is it not the one who reclines at table? But I am among you as the one who serves." (Luke 22:27)*

On that very night Jesus had risen from the table, wrapped a towel around Himself, and washed the disciples' feet. No more moving explanation of Christ's view of leadership could be given than that scene (John 13:1-17). The eternal model of leadership for redeemed men on earth is the incarnate Servant of God, Jesus Christ.

The character of Christian leadership has been captured in the following words of Thomas M. Lindsay, a Scottish theologian of the last century:

> "Everywhere service and leadership go together. These two thoughts are continually associated with a third, that of gifts; for the qualifications which fit a man for service and therefore for rule within the Church of Christ are always looked upon as special gifts of the Spirit of God, or *charismata*. Thus we have three thoughts of qualifications, which is the 'gift' of God; the service to the Church of Christ which these gifts enable those who possess them to perform; and lastly the promise that such service is honoured by the Father, and is the basis for leadership or rule within the Church of Christ."[2]

The privilege of oversight in the family of God comes to those who serve their brethren gladly and selflessly. They demonstrate their divine appointment to rule by the exercise of those gifts given by the Holy Spirit. When leadership becomes isolated from the concept of ministry it is less than Biblical. The association of sanctification and service produces wholesome leaders. The abilities of the pastor, the lay elders and deacons should be the gifts of the Holy Spirit. The human understanding

13

of leadership is one of power and authority. Jesus denied neither of these prerogatives of leadership, in fact, He conferred both power and authority on the leaders He selected. But Christ was careful to explain to His disciples that a true leader is a servant. Inherent in the image of a servant is humility, submission, devotion, sacrifice, a concern for the welfare of those being served.

The Responsibility of Leadership

Leadership at any level which does not seek to find the gifts of the Spirit in the family of believers and cultivate the use of those gifts does not really understand its role. Christ has given every believer a gift for ministry to the whole body. The believer who has never learned to serve Christ and his brethren by exercising his gift is not yet mature. The preaching, teaching, shepherding, and oversight of official leadership should encourage every believer to be a functioning member of the body of Christ.

Not every Christian is a leader, but every Christian is to minister. The essence of Paul's statement to the Ephesian church is this great principle; the work of leadership is to equip all the brotherhood for ministry. To the extent this is achieved by any congregation it will grow.

> . . . *some as pastors and teachers, for the equipping of the saints for the work of service, to the building up of the body of Christ. (Eph. 4:11b-12)*

Activating the potential for ministry in their present membership could revolutionize many churches. Spirit-endowed workers could fill the many ministry needs of the church. When a believer learns to exercise his gift the work assignment becomes a blessed ministry rather than a drag. The success of evangelism, Christian education, the maturation of believers, discipleship, outreach, stewardship, ministry to the community, and prayer all depend on an adequate work force in the church. In the average evangelical church about ten percent of the potential work force is activated. It staggers the mind to anticipate what would happen if even fifty percent of the work force in

14

a congregation would begin to function.

Leadership can either paralyze the work force or prepare it for action. Pastoral and lay leadership can be guilty of making spectators rather than a work force for ministry. Many churches suffer spiritual loss and go into decline because of the failure of their leadership to understand that they should be preparing every believer to minister. A kind of spiritual paternalism develops in some churches. This condition could be compared to a parent who performs a work assignment given a child rather than patiently insisting that the child do the task.

If the leadership carries out its responsibilities with an authoritarian mentality, the initiative of gifted believers in the church will be stifled. Authoritarian leadership feels threatened by the fresh, creative, and sometimes spontaneous ministries which emerge from the membership. A leadership with Biblical understanding welcomes the ministry of the whole body. It seeks to encourage and guide this wonderful life force toward the building up of the body. When pastor, elders, and deacons have this perception of leadership the whole assembly can know the joy of ministering for Christ.

A Basic Leadership Core

The key to activating the congregation to assume ministry is to have a basic core of leaders, composed of the pastor, the elders, and the deacons. They must be committed to teaching, training, and overseeing the believers in their work for Christ. Priority should be given to making the leadership core strong.

Inability to mobilize believers for their ministry is largely due to the failure of the core leadership to understand their function in the body.

Respect for Leadership

The New Testament speaks not only to the issue of the proper attitude on the part of leadership toward the congregation, but it speaks equally to the attitude of the assembly toward leadership. It is important to honor the office God has given to some of His servants. This is a spiritual issue. Lay leaders who find it

15

difficult to give honor to the pastor's position will no doubt find that the congregation will not honor their position as elders and deacons.

Too many contemporary Christians deal with their relationships with others in a purely humanistic manner. But it must be remembered that such thinking is built upon basic presuppositions that are more conformed to modern behavioral sciences than to the revealed Word of God. Respect for the authority of leadership has been challenged by many in modern culture.

God elects to elevate some as servants and requires the others to both respect and honor their position of leadership. Paul taught believers to observe this principle as members of society.

> *Render to all what is due them: tax to whom tax is due; custom to whom custom; fear to whom fear; honor to whom honor. (Rom. 13:7)*

It hardly seems reasonable that if it is a Christian's duty to show respect in the ordinary social situation that such respect would not be observed in the life of the church. Paul spoke to this issue when he said,

> *"But we request of you, brethren, that you appreciate those who diligently labor among you, and have charge over you in the Lord and give you instruction,*
> *"and that you esteem them very highly in love because of their work. Live in peace with one another." (1 Thess. 5:12-13)*

The writer of the Epistle to the Hebrews admonishes the Christian community to give regard to those over them in the Lord.

> *"Obey your leaders, and submit to them; for they keep watch over your souls, as those who will give an account. Let them do this with joy and not with grief, for this would be unprofitable for you." (Heb. 13:17)*

This passage suggests that the attitude of a Christian to his

16

God-appointed leaders has far-reaching implications. A mutuality of regard is the law of relationship in the New Testament church.

---

[1] Richard L. Dresselhaus, *The Deacon and His Ministry*, Gospel Publishing House, Springfield, Missouri, 1977, p. 9.

[2] Thomas M. Lindsay, *The Church and the Ministry in the Early Centuries*, Klock and Klock Christian Publishers, Minneapolis, reprint 1977 (originally published by George H. Doran Company, New York, about 1881), pp. 63, 64.

2

Who Is the Pastor?

A pastor is a shepherd. The shepherd watches over, feeds, protects, and leads a flock of sheep. The leaders of God's people are frequently called shepherds in the Old Testament. The prophets in speaking to the leaders of Israel addressed them as shepherds.

The Lord Jesus saw the absence of true shepherds as the underlying cause of Israel's spiritual condition at the time of His earthly ministry. Looking on a multitude of needy people, Jesus was deeply moved. Matthew said,

> *"And seeing the multitude, He felt compassion for them, because they were distressed and downcast like sheep without a shepherd." (Matt. 9:36)*

Being without a shepherd is an abnormal situation that leaves sheep vulnerable and devastated. Every gathering of the Lord's people has a similar need for a shepherd gifted by Christ to feed and watch over them.

Christ is the Pastor of all pastors. He is called the good shepherd,[1] the great shepherd,[2] and the chief shepherd.[3] Peter describes Christ as the shepherd of our soul.[4] Though Christ has ascended on high, He is still the chief Pastor of the church on earth. His plan for shepherding the church calls for under-shepherds who directly and immediately care for the flock of God.

The concept of the pastor or shepherd was more clearly revealed as the New Testament was written. Paul, under inspiration, wrote of the church leaders whose responsibility it was to equip the church for her work of ministry.

> *"And He gave some as apostles, and some as prophets,*

19

and some as evangelists, and some as pastors and teachers." (Eph. 4:11)

The pastor is one of the gifted men the church needs for the
equipping of the saints and for the building up of the body. He is
a member of that body called to minister to the body.

Two Classes of Elders

The association of the eldership with the pastoral office developed early in the history of the church. When Paul gathered
the elders from Ephesus at Miletus to bid them farewell he gave
a most comprehensive statement on the work of elders.

> *Be on guard for yourselves and for all the flock, among
> which the Holy Spirit has made you overseers, to shepherd
> the church of God which He purchased with His own blood.
> (Acts 20:28)*

Another important reference to this association is found in the
writings of the apostle Peter:

> *Therefore I exhort the elders among you, as your fellow-
> elder and witness of the sufferings of Christ, and a partaker
> also of the glory that is to be revealed,*
> *shepherd the flock of God among you, not under compul-
> sion, but voluntarily, according to the will of God; and not for
> sordid gain, but with eagerness;*
> *nor yet as lording it over those allotted to your charge, but
> proving to be examples to the flock (1 Pet. 5:1-3)*

Both Paul and Peter assign the pastoral responsibility to elders. Since a plurality of elders is the norm in the New Testament church, are all elders equally pastors or are some elders set
apart to be pastors? The answer comes from an examination of
all that the New Testament says about elders. The fact that
Peter identifies himself as an elder and that the apostle John also
calls himself an elder would in itself indicate that there is more
than one class of elders in the New Testament.
The New Testament speaks of two kinds of elders. Peter and

20

John were apostles, yet they were elders. The pastor whose oversight of the assembly includes the elders is referred to as an elder. The Presbyterian system refers to teaching elders and ruling elders. However, a careful study of the scripture passages dealing with eldership raises a question as to these designations. There appears to be an overlapping of duties, and elders are not neatly divided into those who rule and those who teach.

The key passage for this consideration is 1 Tim. 5:17-19:

> *Let the elders who rule well be considered worthy of double honor, especially those who work hard at preaching and teaching.*
>
> *For the Scripture says, "You shall not muzzle the ox while he is threshing," and "The laborer is worthy of his wages."*
>
> *Do not receive an accusation against an elder except on the basis of two or three witnesses.*

The elders described here have these distinctions:

1. They rule well.
2. They deserve double honor.
3. They work hard at both preaching and teaching.
4. They receive remuneration for their work.

It seems that this description fits the pastoral role. The pastor is an elder who both rules and teaches. He is an elder who is elevated to the position of pastor because of his gifts and his commitment. This is recognized by the church in the act of ordination. In 1 Thess. 5:12-13 Paul rounds out his understanding of the pastor-elder.

> *But we request of you, brethren, that you appreciate those who diligently labor among you, and have charge over you in the Lord and give you instruction,*
>
> *and that you esteem them very highly in love because of their work. Live in peace with one another.*

He was to be appreciated, esteemed, and loved by the brotherhood for his diligent labors among the saints. Again in this passage the responsibility of instruction is coupled with the charge to give oversight to the assembly.

The pastor-elder is the undershepherd responsible for both the spiritual and the administrative oversight of the congregation.

Dr. Simpson held to the conviction that there were two kinds of elders in the early church. Simpson saw a distinction between the pastor-elder and the lay-elder.

"The Apostle gives us in these pastoral epistles a good many glimpses of church government in the early church. It is evident that the principal official ministers in the church at Ephesus were elders and deacons. It is also evident that the words *elders* and *bishop* were used interchangeably and that they both denote an office of spiritual oversight. A little later there is a distinction in I Timothy 5:17 between two classes of elders, the one that seems only to have exercised authority and rule, the other class who 'labor in the Word of doctrine.' In other words, the one was a ruling elder, the other a teaching elder."[5]

The Jerusalem Model

The first assembly of the church age was at Jerusalem. Its unusual growth under the outpouring of the Holy Spirit is recorded in Acts. At its inception the apostle Peter was the obvious leader and spokesman of the congregation. The sixth chapter of Acts details the selection of deacons to supplement the leadership of the Apostles. No mention is made of elders at the beginning of the work. This is probably due to the composition of the church. As a totally Jewish congregation many of its converts were elders, and they continued to minister as such in the new body of believers.

As the apostles scattered in the missionary labors the elders took on prominence in the Jerusalem church. They are first mentioned in Acts 11:30:

And this they did, sending it in charge of Barnabas and Saul to the elders.

The first indication of a new leader for the Jerusalem church can be found in the next chapter of Acts. Peter, assisted by an angel, had escaped from prison. He went to a gathering of believers in the home of Mary, the mother of John Mark, and directed the Christians to report this matter to James and the brethren. The implication of this instruction was that James served as the recognized leader of the church. Peter's message to the elders was to go through James, their leader and spokesman.

Bishop Lightfoot, an Anglican whose scholarly treatment of the Christian ministry is considered a classic, captures the significance of James' position in the following comments:

"From this it may be inferred that though holding a position superior to the rest, he was still considered as a member of the presbytery; that he was in fact the head or president of the college."[6]

Charles E. Brown, theologian at Anderson Theological Seminary of the Church of God, underscores the practical meaning of James' position.

"The position of James in the Church at Jerusalem as previously pointed out is unequivocal circumstantial evidence indicating his position of leadership as bishop or pastor of that church, and this is the title given him by the early church historians. Acts 15:13; 21:18 and Galatians 1:19, along with still other texts, indicate clearly his position of leadership in the Jerusalem congregation."[7]

The conclusions of John Kennedy, Plymouth Brethren writer and missionary to India, about James' leadership is significant.

". . . It is, of course, necessary, that when the need arises, one of the company of elders should act as spokesman for the group (it is hardly practical that all should speak in unison), but James ultimately occupied a position which was much more than this. He becomes more even than first among equals; he became first pure and simple, and emerged distinctly as leader of the group."[8]

These writers are concluding that James came to a place of

leadership in this, the first Christian assembly that can be considered the equivalent of the pastor's leadership in a contemporary evangelical church.

The distinct kind of leadership exercised by James with apostolic approval altered the concept of a plurality of elders. The eldership, even at this early stage, called for a class of elders commissioned to the pastoral ministry.

The Distinguishing Marks of the Pastor-Elder

The pastor-elder and the lay-elder differ in *vocation*. The pastor-elder is a full-time minister of the gospel. He has abandoned secular labor to devote full time to the oversight and instruction of the church. The lay-elder is engaged in a secular vocation and ministers as an elder as time permits.

The pastor-elder and the lay-elder differ in responsibility. The pastor is the constituted shepherd of the flock. He is to faithfully preach and teach the Word. He has oversight over all the ministries of the local church. He is responsible to train the lay leadership of the church. As pastor he keeps informed on every aspect of the congregation's ministry. He is a member ex-officio of all boards and committees so that he may be informed of all aspects of the work and so that he may give necessary administrative counsel.

The pastor-elder differs from the lay-elder in that he has had special training for his ministry. The pastoral candidate receives a theological education which provides him with tools for the study of the Scripture and the proclamation of Biblical truth. Those men called late in life and therefore unable to enter an academic program receive basic theological training under the guidance of the district ordaining council. Today's pastor has a minimum of four years of formal education for the ministry. The majority have seven years of undergraduate and graduate training. In addition to his formal training he must have a two-year period of in-service training before ordination. He is examined by the ordaining council as to his doctrine, his Christian experience, and his call to the ministry.

The gifts of a pastor may differ from those of the lay-elders in his congregation. The Holy Spirit distributes gifts as He sees the need of an office or ministry. Paul says this of the pastoral gifts.

Do not neglect the spiritual gift within you, which was bestowed upon you through prophetic utterance with the laying on of hands by the presbytery.

Take pains with these things; be absorbed in them, so that your progress may be evident to all.

Pay close attention to yourself and to your teaching; persevere in these things; for as you do this you will insure salvation both for yourself and for those who hear you. (1 Tim. 4:14-16)

This admonition to Timothy is applicable to the modern pastor, instructing those who proclaim the Word of God to the congregation. As the pastor exercises his spiritual gifts by hard work and faithful devotion his ministry is blessed of God.

The ability for pastoral administration is also God-given. It can be improved upon by the faithful use of that gift under the guidance of the Holy Spirit. The brethren chosen for pastoral ministry need the gift of being the head of the congregation. Such a gift is available according to Romans 12:8:

. . . he who leads with diligence

The Greek word *proistamenous* is translated "leads" in this text. The lexicon gives the following meanings for *proistamenous*.

"Be at the head (of), rule, direct."[9]

The same Greek word is found in 1 Thess. 5:12 where it is translated "have charge over." Paul used this word again in 1 Tim. 5:17 where it is translated "rule." The apostle considered the gift of being a good leader essential to that class of elders called to be pastor.

Leon Morris, the distinguished Anglican scholar, is convinced that the gift of ruling applies to office-bearing leadership within the church. Morris says of this gift in his comments on 1 Thess. 5:17:

"Them that 'are over you in the Lord' is not an official description of a technical order of ministry, but it is difficult to see who could be meant other than the office-bearers in the church. The verb may be used of informal leadership, but it is also an official word, describing the function of those who are officers. The addition of 'in the Lord' also seems to point us to office-bearing in the church, while, at the same time, it adds the idea of the spiritual fitness of things. This is not a cold, external authority but one exercised in the warmth of Christian bonds. Being 'in the Lord' it is an authority to be exercised for the spiritual good of believers (2 Cor. 10:8), and not to give office-bearers opportunity for lording it over them (Luke 22:25)."[10]

The Protestant Tradition

The Protestant tradition of a pastor serving as the leading officer of the congregation has scriptural precedent. It has abundant support in the earliest documents of the post-apostolic church. The Reformers sought to correct the abuses of ecclesiastical power that had so long characterized the institutional church. Luther, Calvin, and Zwingli were not so unwise as to abandon church organization because it had become corrupt. They searched the Scriptures to rediscover a Biblical simplicity in church government. The reformers found the pastor to be the principal leader with lay leaders commissioned by the church to assist and support the work.

The pastoral role in most evangelical churches corresponds to the principle and spirit of leadership found in the first century church. It allows for a team of leaders, but insists that for the sake of order a single chief leader is necessary.

A hierarchical or totalitarian attitude by a pastor is a contradiction of the true spirit of this office. The pastor is servant as are all the leaders in Christ's church, he is a member of the body, he is an elder. The pastor-elder assumes his responsible role as leader with no feeling of superiority. Donald J. MacNair, a Reformed Presbyterian Mission executive, brings into focus the pastor's relationship to the elders and the whole assembly in very understandable terms:

"Paul relates the offices of ruling elder and pastor-teacher by declaring that both are essentially ruling elders (1 Tim.

5:17), but that the pastor-teacher has a special calling, obligation, and privilege of service among his peers (that is, among the ruling elders). From this it is evident that there is, at least, a special category among the ruling elders for the special office of ruling-teaching elder. And this special office will demand special training, examination and financing; it also demands an inherent necessity for special ability to lead people."[11]

In order for the pastoral ministry to be effective the supportive leaders of the local church must understand and allow for the prerogatives of a pastor-elder leadership. Nothing about this system infers that pastors are employees of the church. They are elders placed in the pastoral role by the church under the direction of the Holy Spirit. When both the pastor-elder and the lay-elders understand this working principle the ground work has been laid for rich interaction as fellow elders in the church of God.

---

[1] John 10:14

[2] Hebrews 13:20

[3] 1 Peter 5:4

[4] 1 Peter 2:25

[5] A. B. Simpson, *The Epistle of Thessalonians, Timothy, and Titus,* Christian Publications, Harrisburg, Pa., p. 68.

[6] J. B. Lightfoot, *The Christian Ministry,* MacMillan and Co., London, 1901, p. 26.

[7] Charles Ewing Brown, *The Church Beyond Division,* The Warner Press, Anderson, Indiana, 1946, p. 193.

[8] John Kennedy, *The Torch of the Testimony,* Gospel Literature Service, Bombay, 1961, p. 50.

[9] W. F. Arndt and F. W. Gingrich, *A Greek Lexicon of the New Testament and Other Early Christian Literature,* The University of Chicago Press, Chicago, 1974, p. 713.

[10] Leon Morris, *The New International Commentary, The First and Second Epistles to the Thessalonians,* William B. Erdman, Grand Rapids, 1959, p. 166.

[11] Donald J. MacNair, *The Growing Local Church,* Baker Book House, Grand Rapids, Michigan, 1973, pp. 36, 37.

3

Who Are the Elders?

The office of elder is perhaps the oldest existent form of community leadership having a written history from the days of Israel's patriarchs. Yet the eldership is as relevant today in the community of believers as it was four thousand years ago. Who are the elders? Why are they so important? The eldership is not just a product of social evolution but a divinely revealed concept of leadership among God's people.

The first mention of an elder in the Bible is found in Genesis 24:2:

> *And Abraham said to his servant, the oldest of his household, who had charge of all that he owned, . . .*

Abraham had an elder to oversee his household. This passage points up the root meaning of eldership, simply one who is old. The emphasis is not on his age per se. The usage infers that the older one is assuming oversight because he has wisdom and experience. In the society of Abraham age was respected because the culture had learned that mature judgment was the product of long experience. Mature men were chosen to rule in such a society. Maturity not only physiologically, but maturity spiritually and intellectually entitled them to leadership.

Eldership in the Nation of Israel

By the time Abraham's family had developed into twelve tribes the eldership was a fixed office in the government of ancient Israel. When Moses was commissioned by Jehovah to deliver Israel from Egyptian bondage he contacted the elders of Israel. His first ministry upon returning to Egypt was to assemble the elders of Israel and make known to them Jehovah's word. (Exodus 4:29)

The office of elder in Israel stood along side the seer, the prophet, and the priest. In the theocracy of God's ancient people the elders had the oversight of smaller units within the whole of Israel. Their responsibility was governmental, social, and spiritual.

The eldership increased in importance as Israel began her wilderness experience. The administrative load Moses had to carry was too much for him so he sought the Lord for some relief from this pressure. The Lord gave him the following instructions.

> . . . "Gather for Me seventy men from the elders of Israel, whom you know to be the elders of the people and their officers and bring them to the tent of meeting, and let them take their stand there with you.
> "Then I will come down and speak with you there, and I will take of the Spirit who is upon you, and will put him upon them; and they shall bear the burden of the people with you, so that you shall not bear it all alone." (Num. 11:16-17)

The dignity and divine approval of the eldership was forever established by this sacred event. The elders were anointed by the Holy Spirit to share the office of spiritual oversight. A very basic principle was also established when God gathered the seventy elders before His presence. In setting them apart to share the burden God brought into His house the important dimension of supportive leadership. Moses was a stronger leader because seventy Spirit-touched men would bear the burden with him. Effectiveness and efficiency were the outcome of the co-ministry of the elders of Israel. Moses was no less a leader than before. The elders did not compound his problems by their own innovations but together with Moses they cared for and shepherded the family of God.

The concept of elders gradually enlarged across the years of Old Testament history. The centuries brought enrichment to the office. The foundation was being laid in the Old Testament for eldership in the New Testament church. Its antecedents were all found in Israel. Tracing the path of the elders over the ages of Israel's experience reveals a very full picture of eldership.

When Moses smote the rock in Horeb from which God brought a copious stream of water, the scriptures say that he did so in the sight of the elders of Israel. He was given in Exodus 17:5 explicit instructions to take the elders with him, for they were to be co-witnesses of the supernatural act which brought water out of a flinty rock. This passage offers interesting insight into the function of eldership in Israel.

Closely related to the incident at the rock was the prominence of the elders at the confirming of the covenant found in Exodus 24. Jehovah again instructs Moses to bring the priest, Aaron and his sons, and the elders to witness the divine manifestation and the divine revelation of the words of the Lord.

> *Then Moses went up with Aaron, Nadab and Abihu, and seventy of the elders of Israel, and they saw the God of Israel; and under His feet there appeared to be a pavement of sapphire, as clear as the sky itself. Yet He did not stretch out His hand against the nobles of the sons of Israel; and they beheld God, and they ate and drank. (Ex. 24:9-11)*

It is evident that the seventy elders knew the spiritual realities Moses had come to know. Their firsthand knowledge of the glory, power, and holiness of Jehovah was an essential preparation for their responsibility in the camp of God's people.

The elders of Israel were the most enduring form of leadership in Israel. Prophets came and went as spiritual tides would rise and fall. Judges and kings were not always enduring. The priesthood in times of spiritual decline fell into disrepute. In the dark and terrible days of the judges time and again the only credible leadership that remained was the elders.

At the final collapse of Israel as a nation the eldership survived even in captivity. The temple lay in ruins, the gates of the holy city burned with fire, her people were in captivity in a strange land—nothing of the structure of Israel remained. Even in those days of suffering God's people had elders to lead and console them. During this period the elders of Israel did their greatest service, moving among the broken and confused refu-

31

gees, praying and teaching, which eventually revived Israel again.

Separated from the altar in Jerusalem the priests in Israel could offer no sacrifice. Cut off from the rich blessing of this sacrificial system, God's people turned to the spiritual exercise of prayer and Bible study. Small groups gathered to hear the Word expounded by elders who had become scribes, men noted for their ability to explain the Word of God. During those years the scattered believers learned to assemble with the Bible as the center of their interest.

A pattern developed in Israel that was to stay with the nation even after their return to the land. The reconstruction of the temple and the restoration of the Levitical sacrifices would not distract them from the new structure they had discovered in captivity. The small neighborhood assemblies continued, and the new and enlarged role of the elder also continued. Elders had become teachers and proclaimers of Biblical doctrine. This important historical development was to have a bearing on the life of the church Christ would found. By the time the Messiah came Jewish synagogues were to be found in every village. The concept of assemblies for prayer and learning so central to the New Testament Church had already been born in the spiritual experience of Israel.

Elders in the Hebrew Church

There were many elders in Palestine in the days of Christ. The frequent mention of elders in the four Gospels indicates the importance of their leadership in each community. The temple sacramental worship in Jerusalem was directed by priests from the tribe of Levi, but the simple assemblies for worship and study of the scripture was carried on in each village synagogue by a group of elders.

The Jewish elders would select one of their number to be the president of the synagogue. It was his responsibility to preside at meetings and to be the official spokesman for the group. The elders not only ruled the congregation but they also ministered to them by teaching the scriptures. The theology of Judaism by this time had lost much of its vitality. A complete legalism had taken over in the religious life of Israel. It must be remembered that every reference to elders in the four Gospels have to do with Jewish elders.

The first Christian elder is mentioned in Acts 11:30. The apostles had been placed as leaders in the Jerusalem church and deacons had been appointed to care for the material needs of the Hellenistic Jews. The Acts does not record the ordination of the first Christian elders in Jerusalem. No doubt many of the early converts to Christ were former Jewish elders. It was quite natural for their recognized leaders and opinion-makers to become leaders in the assembly of their new-found faith. For some years after Pentecost the entire Christian community was Jewish. The spread of the gospel through Judea, Samaria and Galilee is a remarkable record of church planting. As new churches were established an eldership emerged in each assembly. The pattern of an eldership to oversee the assembly was culturally acceptable and it obviously had divine approval.

Elders in the Gentile Church

When the evangelistic outreach of the Palestinian church began among the Gentiles the eldership was carried by the missionaries throughout the Roman world. The apostle Paul did not consider his work complete in any new church until a viable eldership had been commissioned to oversee the work.

> *And when they had appointed elders for them in every church, having prayed with fasting, they commended them to the Lord in whom they had believed. (Acts 14:23)*

Paul and his missionary associates would allow some time after the initial conversion of the group before selecting the elders. Time was allowed for growth in these new Christians since the leadership was to be chosen from the congregation. The brethren with gifts for leadership would begin to demonstrate their abilities. The credibility of their spiritual life would be established by this time. At a subsequent visit to the new church the elders were set apart to minister.

The term elder was not entirely strange to the Gentile cities where early Christian missionaries planted churches. It had a secular meaning in the Gentile culture. Deissman, New Testament Greek scholar, found that in the Greek vernacular the term elder was a common designation for a ruler of a corporation in the provinces of Asia Minor. When Paul appointed elders in Derbe, Lystra, and Iconium the new Christians which made up those churches would have understood from their own culture that eldership was an official position in the church.

The growth of the church required the refinement of her forms to meet the new functions. Before the close of the first century the complexity of church life called for a greater emphasis on the pastor-elder role in the church.

During the formative period of rapid and widespread church planting the administration pattern followed a plurality of elders. The development of the church saw the president or presiding elder become the pastor.

Elders and Bishops

The use of two terms *bishop* and *elder* lends support to the idea that two classes of elders existed in the apostolic church. In Paul's address to the Ephesian elders he called them bishops—they were overseers, their responsibility was administrative. Their is historical evidence that a pattern emerged in the early church in which one bishop was appointed to serve as the principle overseer of the church.

The word *bishop* is found only in the preaching or writings of the apostle Paul. Paul used the term as synonymous with the term elder. Scholars agree that bishops were elders. The question must be raised whether all elders were bishops as well. Paul's usage of this term *bishop* in the Pastoral Epistles suggests that this term could apply to certain elders. He spoke in particular of the elders who both taught and gave oversight to the church, namely, the pastor-elder. The term *bishop* seems to fit with the pastoral responsibility.

Whatever simplistic organizational structures were initially employed in the apostolic churches by the time Paul wrote his instructions to Timothy and Titus he had received divine guidance in the matter of church order. He speaks of bishops, elders,

34

and deacons as officers of the church.

The office of the bishop as distinct among the elders is supported by Kittel's conclusion on the first chapter of Titus.

"It is thus natural to suppose that the offices are one (bishop and elders) and the same in the Pastorals. Only thus can one explain the fact that just after Titus is told to appoint elders (1:5) the portrait of a bishop is given (vv 7 ff.). Yet one can hardly make a complete equation. This is proved by the simple fact that in the Pastorals *episkopos* is always in the singular while the *presbuteroi* form a college."[1]

There is evidence that before the close of the apostolic age the church had come to recognize three offices in the local church. This assumption is strengthened by the pattern of officials described in the earliest existent written documents outside of the scriptures. *The Teaching of the Twelve Apostles, Apostolic Canons,* and *The Letters of Ignatius of Antioch* were all written before 180 A.D. *The Teachings of the Twelve Apostles* has been dated by some scholars at 100 A.D.

The gradual change of the Gentile churches from a twofold ministry to a threefold ministry is summarized by Thomas M. Lindsay.

"The change made consisted in placing at the head of this college of rulers one man, who was commonly called either the pastor or the bishop, the latter name being the more usual, and apparently the technical designation. The ministry of each congregation or local church instead of being, as it had been, two-fold—of elders and deacons—became threefold—of pastor or bishop, elders and deacons. This was the introduction of what is called the three-fold ministry. It is commonly called the beginning of episcopacy; but that idea is based on the erroneous conception that a three-fold ministry and episcopacy are identical."[2]

As the Gentile churches grew and matured they followed the precedent of the Palestinian churches in adopting the form of a pastor, elders and deacons as the norm for leadership.

The threefold ministry persisted in the church until the Roman hierarchical system modified it. As the Roman Catholic church made the pastor a priest the role of eldership became less significant. In time of multiple eldership in the local church became non-existent. The Protestant reformation saw the restoration of the eldership. Priests became pastors and lay-elders were instituted once again to give supportive leadership with their fellow elder, the pastor.

The Function of the Lay-elder

The management of the spiritual and material needs of any growing church is an extensive responsibility. One man cannot effectively carry out all functions implied in pastoral oversight. The pastor is the coordinator and general overseer of the work, but he must have supportive leaders to rightly carry out his function. To be chosen as a lay-elder is much more than an honor conferred by the congregation upon some faithful member. It is a calling. It is a ministry absolutely essential to the welfare of any local church. The lay-elders help the pastor with the task of oversight and with the shepherding of the flock of God.

As did the ancient elders in Israel so the modern elder will, to the extent of his gifts and assignments, help rule and care for the congregation. Multiple-eldership is a divine plan for expanding the work force of the local church. Only as the workers increase in number can the church grow numerically. Undershepherds working with the pastor-elder make possible a high level of people-centered pastoral care for even the largest church.

In many evangelical churches today the eldership is little more than an honor guard. Modern evangelicals do well to restudy the writings of the reformation on this subject. The newer denominations in particular have been derelict in establishing a truly New Testament church order. The renewal of lay participation in the assembly calls for a fresh consideration of the ancient but relevant ministry of lay elders.

---

[1] Kittle's Word Studies, Vol 6, pp. 662-680

[2] Thomas M. Lindsay, *The Church and the Ministry in the Early Centuries,* Klock and Klock Christian Publisher, Minneapolis (1977 reprint), p. 170.

4

Who Are the Deacons?

The work of a deacon has often been defined as the trusteeship of the material aspects of the church. A broad spectrum of job descriptions are assigned them under this definition. Some churches give to the deacons the responsibility of collecting and distributing the benevolences of the church. Others make them the custodians of the properties of the assembly. Still others see the *diaconate* as accounting for the business and financial matters of the congregation.

Among Baptist churches the deacons are often assigned to the work that other church bodies give to the elders.

None of these systems seem to have a broad enough horizon for the *diaconate* when compared with the New Testament scriptures. It does not appear that they had the oversight of the church since that fell to the elders. However, the work of a deacon went beyond waiting on tables. One of few recorded sermons in the Book of Acts is by Stephen, the deacon, delivered before the highest Jewish executive body. He preached with power and skill. Another deacon driven from his home by persecution was God's instrument for the planting of a great church. The scriptures are careful to record an incident of his ability as a personal soul-winner. Every modern deacon should read Acts 8:26-40 and ask God to use him to win other men to Christ as Philip did.

The Meaning of the Word *Deacon*

The Greek word for deacon, *diakonos,* means one who serves or ministers. It applied to a household slave who waited on tables. Like many other words in the vernacular of that time the New Testament lifted this word *diakonos* to a much higher meaning. The *diakonos* of the New Testament church was a

37

minister of compassion officially appointed by the church. He held a place of dignity in the assembly. His ministry was supportive of the pastoral leadership and that of the lay elders.

The Origin of Deaconship

The scriptures have preserved the record of the origin of the *diaconate* or deaconship.

> *And in those days, when the number of the disciples was multiplied, there arose a murmuring of the Grecians against the Hebrews, because their widows were neglected in the daily ministration. Then the twelve called the multitude of the disciples unto them, and said, It is not reason that we should leave the word of God, and serve tables. Wherefore, brethren, look ye out among you seven men of honest report, full of the Holy Ghost and wisdom, whom we may appoint over this business. But we will give ourselves continually to prayer, and to the ministry of the word. And the saying pleased the whole multitude: and they chose Stephen, a man full of faith and of the Holy Ghost, and Philip, and Prochorus, and Nicanor, and Timon, and Parmenas, and Nicolas a proselyte of Antioch: When they set before the apostles: and when they had prayed, they laid their hands on them. (Acts 6:1-6—KJV)*

The seven deacons chosen by the Jerusalem church were necessary to the welfare and growth of that great church. Deacons were selected to enlarge and to specialize the work force. They were to apply their gifts and wisdom to the social needs of the assembly in order to free the preaching staff from the details involved in such ministry.

Acts not only gives the genesis of the deaconship but also gives some essential insights into the qualities of deacons as well. The manner of selecting and consecrating the deacons in this first church verify the importance of the office.

Some Bible scholars are persuaded that even before the appointment of the seven an order of servants existed in the church which finally emerged as the deaconship. The scripture sighted for this is Acts 5:6. In the account of the remarkable judgment on Ananias and Sapphira, the young men were summoned to remove the bodies from the place of assembly. *Neoteroi* translated "young" may refer to the first deacon, suggested by the use of this term in Luke 22:26.

> *And there was also a strife among them, which of them should be accounted the greatest. And he said unto them, The kings of the Gentiles exercise lordshop over them; and they that exercise authority upon them are called benefactors. But ye shall not be so: but he that is greatest among you, let him be as the younger; and he that is chief, as he that doth serve. (Luke 22:24-26—KJV)*

Christ was suggesting such a ministry to be a part of the leadership of the church. *Neoteroi* carried such a meaning in Greek usage.

The church in Jerualsem provides an excellent model for the development of the elders and deacons. This new order of ministry was created to meet the leadership needs of that growing congregation. The guidance of the Holy Spirit was sought in the forming of the office and in the selection of men to fill that office.

The Jerusalem church by active and continuous evangelism had won to Christ scores of Hellenistic Jews as well as Aramaic-speaking Jews. The new assembly soon discovered tension developing between these two ethnic groups. The peculiar circumstances under which the church ministered added to the problem. Fanatic persecution from the non-Christian community had left many believers totally destitute. More fortunate members were willing to make great sacrifices of their material wealth so that the needy in the Christian community might be adequately cared for. The pressure of feeding hundreds of people each day produced problems. The apostolic leaders were guided by the Holy Spirit to resolve these problems by adding to the church's work force the *diaconate* or the deacons.

By the end of the apostolic period the office of deacon was well established in the life of the church. It has survived until modern times and is currently reaching a new place of importance in the ministry of the church.

The Cultural Background of the *Diaconate*

The Greek word, *diakonos*, from which we get deacon, means a servant. In the Gentile culture to be a servant was usually to be a slave, a position of inferiority. The only exception to this was when the term occasionally was applied to some form of government service.

The perception of a servant was quite different in Jewish culture. The position of a servant was not considered inferior. In fact to be the servant of a good and great master was thought to be a high honor. The *diaconate* was born in the Jewish churches and probably reflected their understanding of servanthood. As the church grew and crossed cultural lines the *diaconate* survived and increased in importance. The pagan idea of inferiority was not applied to the servants of the church. The deacons of the early church were men of humility but not inferior men. This was an office respected by the church, one extremely important to the well-being of the church.

The Duties of the Office of Deacon

> *Paul and Timothy, bond-servants of Christ Jesus, to all the saints in Christ Jesus who are in Philippi, including the overseers and deacons. (Phil. 1:1)*

By the time Paul wrote his epistle to the Philippians the office of deacon had become firmly established in the church. Paul and Timothy addressed the believers of that assembly and then the office-bearers of the assembly, the bishops and the deacons. These two offices had the administrative responsibilities and no doubt had been the official channel of correspondence with Paul and Timothy. In behalf of the congregation the bishops and deacons had sent funds for the support of Paul's ministry. Hendrich Meyer, German theologian of the nineteenth century, suggests that Paul addressed the leaders in this special way because of the nature of his letter. It was not only an epistle of teaching but it was a thank you letter for their financial support.[1] This would suggest that early Christians had a very sophisticated system of stewardship. Individuals had given their gifts to the church, which had sent the gifts to Paul through their appropriate officers. This would account for the salutation to the church officers only in the letter to the Philippians.

The founder of the Christian and Missionary Alliance, Dr. A. B. Simpson, understood deacons to be significant in the government of the church.

> "There was a second class of officers called deacons. The word denotes a minister; that is, one who ministers—a servant to the church. This sufficiently covers the office of deacon as it is usually exercised today in Christian churches, the ministry of hospitality, kindness to the sick, the stranger, and the sufferer, and relief to the poor and needy. These ministries are so important that the office of deacon was the first to be filled by the apostolic church . . ."[2]

The church during the days of its greatest spiritual power was the most active in ministries of compassion to suffering people. The deacons were responsible for the leadership of this manifestation of love. We are not told in scripture that the *diaconate* of the primitive church ministered to the needy of society in general. The scriptural record relates to the suffering within the church.

But it must be kept in mind that the deacons did more than minister to the poor. The Jerusalem church was under such intense persecution that much of the congregation were suffering poverty. The first seven deacons were set aside to direct the ministry to this needy multitude.

The situation at Philippi was quite different. There is no evidence of poverty there. The congregation was able on more than one occasion to send financial support to the apostle Paul and his missionary team. Yet this church had deacons and they were so prominent as to receive special greetings from Paul. Some scholars have attempted to prove that deacons were elected only in those churches having a problem with poverty. The New Testament data does not support that premise. If deacons were a norm in the churches of that day, their function must have included a larger ministry than was first assigned them in Acts chapter six. While the scriptures provide no examples of the *diaconate* ministering to the physical needs of the non-Christian community this could have been the case in churches where the believers themselves suffered no poverty. The very spirit of Christian charity seems to call for this kind of ministry. It has occurred in the subsequent history of the church again and again.

The duties of the deacon in the days of the apostles was evidently larger than a ministry of waiting on tables. They ministered to spiritual needs as well as to physical needs.

In the post-apostolic period deacons continued to be an essential office of ministry. Clement of Rome, one of the church fathers, in a reference to the spread of the gospel speaks of the continued importance of deacons in his time. He refers to the apostles,

"having received a charge, and having been fully assured through the resurrection of our Lord Jesus Christ and conformed in the Word of God with full assurance of the Holy Ghost, they went forth with the glad tidings that the kingdom of God should come. So preaching everywhere in country and town, they appointed their first fruits, when they had proved them by the Spirit, to be bishops and deacons unto them that should believe."[3]

The duties of a deacon are further amplified by the ministry of Philip, one of the original seven deacons in Jerusalem. Persecution became so intense that Philip along with most of the leaders of the Christian church had to flee Jerusalem for their lives. Philip went north to Samaria and began to preach the gospel.

Therefore, those who had been scattered went about preaching the word.

And Philip went down to the city of Samaria and began proclaiming Christ to them.

And the multitudes with one accord were giving attention to what was said by Philip, as they heard and saw the signs which he was performing.

For in the case of many who had unclean spirits, they were coming out of them shouting with a loud voice; and many who had been paralyzed and lame were healed.

And there was much rejoicing in that city. (Acts 8:4-8)

42

The ministry of Philip in this rather alien community produced a remarkable outpouring of the Holy Spirit. Apparently Philip did not engage in the usual work of deacons, but seeing the spiritual condition of the city he gave himself to preaching Christ. There was such obvious anointing of the Holy Spirit on his preaching that great crowds of people came to hear Philip. He was also used of God to heal the sick and to exorcise demons.

The effect of deacon Philip's preaching was the gathering of a sizable congregation of believers. The church in Jerusalem, hearing of the working of God in Samaria, delegated Peter and John to perfect the faith and order of this new church.

The ministry of Philip not only included successful church planting but he excelled as well in personal evangelism.

> *But an angel of the Lord spoke to Philip saying, "Arise and go south to the road that descends from Jerusalem to Gaza." (This is a desert road.)*
>
> *And he arose and went; and behold, there was an Ethiopian eunuch, a court official of Candace, queen of the Ethiopians, who was in charge of all her treasure; and he had come to Jerusalem to worship.*
>
> *And he was returning and sitting in his chariot, and was reading the prophet Isaiah.*
>
> *And the Spirit said to Philip, "Go up and join this chariot."*
>
> *And when Philip had run up, he heard him reading Isaiah the prophet, and said, "Do you understand what you are reading?"*
>
> *And he said, "Well, how could I, unless someone guides me?" And he invited Philip to come up and sit with him.*
>
> *Now the passage of Scripture which he was reading was this: "He was led as a sheep to slaughter;*
>
> *And as a lamb before its shearer is silent,*
>
> *So He does not open his mouth.*
>
> *In humiliation His judgment was taken away;*
>
> *Who shall relate His generation?*
>
> *For His life is removed from the earth."*
>
> *And the eunuch answered Philip and said, "Please tell me, of whom does the prophet say this? Of himself, or of someone else?"*

43

And Philip opened his mouth, and beginning from this Scripture he preached Jesus to him.

And as they went along the road they came to some water; and the eunuch said, "Look! Water! What prevents me from being baptized?"

And Philip said, "If you believe with all your heart, you may." And he answered and said, "I believe that Jesus Christ is the Son of God."

And he ordered the chariot to stop; and they both went down into the water, Philip as well as the eunuch; and he baptized him.

And when they came up out of the water, the Spirit of the Lord snatched Philip away; and the eunuch saw him no more, but went on his way rejoicing.

But Philip found himself at Azotus; and as he passed through he kept preaching the gospel to all the cities, until he came to Caesarea. (Acts 8:26-40)

Philip, a Spirit-filled man, could sense the leading of the Holy Spirit in his life. The directive to go to the desert was obeyed without hesitation, and there, by divine appointment, Philip met the Ethiopian. What better situation for personal evangelism, a prepared witness and a seeking soul brought together. Personal soul winning after this pattern should be the experience of all church officers and especially the deacons.

Philip so developed his gifts that he became an evangelist. Scripture does not indicate that he gave up the office of deacon, but since the ministry of an evangelist is to the churches at large and the ministry of the deacon to the local assembly, it can be assumed that he accepted the responsibility of the larger office of evangelist.

Stephen enjoyed a leadership role far beyond the management of food distribution among the needy. His spiritual gifts and testimony for Christ brought him into the public eye. So threatening was the spiritual power of this man that the enemies of Christianity had him put to death. The church should remember that the first martyr of the new age was a deacon. This speaks well of the spirituality and significance of that office.

The ability of Stephen to carry on dialogue with the non-

Christian leadership in the community was critical. So skillful were his arguments on the behalf of the gospel of Christ they could not be refuted. Stephen was an able defender of the faith. Though he paid with his life, Stephen, by the grace of God, presented the gospel to the most difficult segment of Judaism.

The *diaconate* then was a feeder of other orders of ministry in the church. Evangelists, elders, pastors came from the ranks of the deacons. The rather low view of this office in some evangelical churches stifles the full usefulness of the *diaconate*.

Donald J. MacNair, executive of the Reformed Presbyterian Church, shatters this traditional view of deacons when he says,

> "One major truth about the service of the deacon comes through this entire study. The original seven were not simply delivery boys. These men were to use their office and the physical resources at their disposal to bring unity back to the local body of believers to do a mighty and spiritual service." [4]

MacNair makes a point of the responsibility of deacons not only to relieve needs but to deal with the underlying causes of those needs. The deacon then must be sensitive, wise, and knowledgeable of scripture to exercise such an important spiritual ministry.

_____

[1] H. W. A. Meyer, *The Epistle of Paul to the Philippians*, T. & T. Clark, Edinburgh, 1875, p. 13.

[2] A. B. Simpson, *The Epistles of Thessalonians, Timothy, and Titus*, Christian Publications, Inc., Harrisburg, p. 69.

[3] Quote from William Lefroy, *The Christian Ministry*, Funk & Wagnalls, London, 1891, p. 140.

[4] Donald J. MacNair, *The Growing Local Church*, Baker Book House, Grand Rapids, 1975, p. 111.

5

The Leadership Team

The core leadership of the local church is comprised of the pastor, the elders, and the deacons. The relationship and interaction among these leaders is of utmost importance to the effective care of the congregation. The relationship of these core leaders to the other leaders of the congregation is equally important. This pattern of leadership calls for a structure within the local church organization which provides for the interaction, cooperation, and integration of all church ministries. The church executive board is the answer to this need. This board is normally composed of the pastor, the elders or, in the event of a separate board of elders, a representative of that board, the deacons or a representative of the deacon board, the trustees, and other corporate officers. The board is sometimes expanded to include other ministries of the congregation.

The Executive Board

The concept of the executive board has been challenged by some contemporary church renewal writers as unscriptural since in their viewpoint it negates the role of eldership. These writers in most instances are approaching eldership from the Darby position of plurality of elders. To be consistent with this theory not only must the executive board be eliminated but the congregation's voice in government as well. It is the conviction of this author that the executive board is consistent with a Biblical view of the role of elders and deacons and necessary for the best level of total church management. The church executive board is a necessity to the leadership functioning as a team. Without a common board the various ministries begin to fracture. They seek priority in the church's program without regard for the whole. They become competitive rather than supportive in their attitude. The congregation is soon rent with unhealthy tensions and every ministry suffers.

The Role of the Executive Board

The role of an executive board is to integrate all church leadership into a team. No one seeks the preeminence but rather seeks the opportunity to serve the other areas of the ministry. At each regular meeting of the executive board reports should be heard from the pastor, the elders, the deacons, the Christian education board, and all other church ministries. The executive board is the ideal forum for integrating each ministry into the whole. Common goals for growth and expansion are worked out. Each ministry makes its contribution to the whole. This method reduces tensions and cultivates a spirit of unity among church leaders.

The pastor benefits from the executive board by receiving the counsel and wisdom of the lay leaders who compose the board. His perception of the needs of the congregation is greatly heightened by sharing the views of leadership at every level in the church's program.

The elders can provide a stronger ministry to the pastor and the care for the spiritual needs of the congregation when they have exposure to the total operation. Deacons ought to be aware of the work of the elders, the building and financial concerns of the church, its evangelism outreach and discipleship programs. The executive board is an ideal setting for keeping all leadership informed as well as coordinating their activities to achieve their common goals.

Overlapping of Functions

A further rationale for the formation of an executive board is found in the multiple function of church officers and the manner in which these functions overlap. Those who advocate a Darby view of plurality of elders contend that the elders care strictly for the spiritual needs and that financial and material needs are under the care of deacons. A careful examination of the New Testament data indicates that no such cleancut dicotomy of function existed. The very first mention of eldership in the Apostolic church relates to their oversight of financial matters. A famine had caused a serious poverty in the Jerusalem church. The church at Antioch collected relief funds for Jerusalem and the province of Judea. The scripture says,

And this they did, sending it in charge of Barnabas and Saul to the elders. (Acts 11:30)

The deacons did more than oversee the food distribution to the widows and the destitute. They engaged in preaching and other forms of evangelism. The functions of elders and deacons overlapped and it cannot be said that elders engaged only in spiritual concerns and deacons in material concerns.

The following quote from W. R. Walker offers a good insight into the matter of relationship among the church leaders.

". . . Their duties merge. If a guess as to the relationship of the two groups be permitted, it would seem that deacons served along with elders, perhaps as understudies, assistants ministering in whatever capacities their talents or opportunities made possible. If this surmise is correct the prevailing custom of having joint meeting of elders, deacons, trustees, etc., as an official board is justified. But there is little scriptural authority for the rather arbitrary division of work, such as assigning spiritual oversight to elders and financial responsibility to the deacons. The chief objection to a separation of 'spiritual oversight' and 'financial planning' is that the two cannot be separated scripturally. Both come within the area of stewardship. One is the stewardship of talent and the other is the stewardship of material things."[1]

Early Church Tradition

It is probably for this very reason that the early church moved rapidly to a common board of elders and deacons. Thomas Lindsay found this pattern in the writings of Ignatius.

"According to the conception of Ignatius, every Christian community ought to have at its head a bishop, a presbyterium

49

or session of elders, and a body of deacons. These constitute its office-bearers to whom jointly and severally, obedience is due. Ignatius regards these three elements as going together to form a whole. . . ."[2]

The earliest available documents on church organization confirm by the second century that there was widespread practice of the leadership pattern observed by Ignatius.

The *Didache* dating to 135 A.D. speaks of a college of church officers including both elders and deacons with a pastor or bishop presiding.

The Legal Aspect

To consider all the implications of church government today the responsibility of the church to abide by state and federal law calls for the appropriate corporate officers. The early church struggled with this problem, so it is not new. Because of Roman law the church could not receive legal recognition. Most nongovernmental organizations registered with the state as confraternities. There was no vehicle for the church in that pagan society to achieve legal status. This may have accounted for the fact that there were no church buildings. This fact is often interpreted as being a deliberate aspect of early church ecclesiology while in reality it was probably for practical reasons. Because the congregation had no legal status it could not own property.

The Jews were able to build synagogues and administer them with government sanction. Julius Caesar had legislated during his reign that the Jewish communities were lawful confraternities. The Christian churches did not enjoy similar legal status until the time of Constantine.

Zephyrinus, bishop of Rome at the end of the second century, was successful in registering the church a burial club. Tertullian in his *Apology* makes a plea that the government grant Christian churches the status of a legal confraternity.[3]

The legal aspect of church life was a concern in the reformation churches. Luther concluded that for security a state church would be best and consequently aligned himself and his followers with government. Calvin and Zwengli maintained a separation between church and state. The anabaptist followed in that tradition. The Anglican church like the Lutheran came under the jurisdiction of the British State.

In North America the settlers were largely refugees fleeing the persecution of state churches in Europe. Therefore, a sharp separation between church and state prevailed in most of North America.

Social and economic forces in today's culture have made it necessary for the church to be incorporated by state or provincial law. Non-profit corporate status is required for a church to own property; to establish a bank account; to enjoy tax free status. Modern churches must carry out the legal requirements of local law to have ethical credibility.

The responsibility of corporation officers are now thrust on the church's official leadership. Trustees are not mentioned in the Bible but most churches have them. In many states and provinces they are required by law. How can the trusteeship of a legal corporation be integrated with the Biblical concepts of church structure? The resolution of this problem has promoted the idea of an executive church board on which all the officers and ministries are represented. Some churches elect to put the trusteeship into the hands of the deacons while others have elected to separate board of trustees and allow that board representation on the executive board.

[1] W. R. Walker, *A Functioning Eldership,* Standard Publishing Company, Cincinnati, 1940, p. 84.

[2] Thomas M. Lindsay, *The Church and the Ministry in the Early Centuries,* Klock and Klock, Minneapolis, (reprint 1977), p. 196.

[3] Ibid., p. 129.

6

The Scriptural Qualifications of Elders

The apostle Paul considered the qualifications of elders to be so important that he devoted two major passages in the pastoral epistles to a discussion of this subject. Local churches are not left to devise their own standards for eldership. The Bible is explicit as to the kind of men God can use in this ministry.

The inspired list of qualifications is all inclusive. More than spiritual qualities are needed. The man chosen to be an elder must be godly, sensible, of good reputation, a family man and capable of leadership. For the purpose of this study the qualifications in First Timothy six and Titus one will be divided into five categories in order to discover the image of an elder as given in scripture.

Paul provides a list of qualifications for the bishop in 1 Tim. 3:1-7

> *It is a trustworthy statement; if any man aspires to the office of overseer, it is a fine work he desires to do.*
> *An overseer, then, must be above reproach, the husband of one wife, temperate, prudent, respectable, hospitable, able to teach,*
> *not addicted to wine or pugnacious, but gentle, uncontentious, free from the love of money.*
> *He must be one who manages his own household well, keeping his children under control with all dignity*
> *(but if a man does not know how to manage his own household, how will he take care of the church of God?);*
> *and not a new convert, lest he become conceited and fall into the condemnation incurred by the devil.*
> *And he must have a good reputation with those outside the church, so that he may not fall into reproach and the snare of the devil.*

The second list is addressed to the elders.

> *For this reason I left you in Crete, that you might set in order what remains, and appoint elders in every city as I directed you,*
> *namely, if any man be above reproach, the husband of one wife, having children who believe, not accused of dissipation or rebellion.*
> *For the overseer must be above reproach as God's steward, not self-willed, not quick-tempered, not addicted to wine, not pugnacious, not fond of sordid gain,*
> *but hospitable, loving what is good, sensible, just, devout, self-controlled,*
> *holding fast the faithful word which is in accordance with the teaching, that he may be able both to exhort in sound doctrine and to refute those who contradict. (Titus 1:5-9)*

Personal Qualities

The Apostle mentions seven personal qualities for an elder, each relating to his character rather than to his abilities or leadership qualities. They are something of an index to his personality. All of these qualities are important to a person engaged in working with other people. They are essential to good relationships.

Titus 1:7 says of the overseers to be appointed by Titus that they are not to be "self-willed." Another possible translation of this word is self-pleasing. He is not to be a man whose actions please himself irrespective of others. The elder is a believer who has abandoned "selfishness" in favor of "selflessness."

Titus was instructed to seek out for the eldership men who were not quick tempered. The frustrations and pressures of a spiritual leader calls for patience. Fits of temper will mar the Lord's servant and take away his effectiveness. Such uncontrolled temper betrays an inner spiritual need that should be cared for prior to assuming the responsibility of an undershepherd in Christ's church. Paul also warns about men who are pugnacious. Fighters do not belong in the eldership. Problems are not resolved by fighting in the house of God.

Paul tells Timothy that elders are to be "gentle" and "uncontentious" (1 Tim. 3:3). In the course of his duties an elder must deal with all kinds of people who need tender, loving care. A man of harsh spirit eliminates himself from such a shepherding ministry.

These qualities are largely related to temperament. Temperament and spirituality cannot be separated. The fruits of the Spirit found in Galatians 5:22-23 describe the characteristics of Christian temperament.

But more than temperament is involved in the scriptural requirements for elders. Conduct is of equal importance. In both letters—to Timothy and to Titus—the apostle Paul makes the point that an elder is not to be addicted to wine. Paul is saying that elders are to be chosen from among those mature believers who have found victory over those habits that are harmful to their person and to their testimony. The elder cannot serve as an example nor can he counsel others if he is compromising the life of holiness by unclean habits.

The list in First Timothy couples the two words *temperate* and *prudent* as necessary personal qualities for this level of leadership. The word *temperate* can mean sober or moderate. The elder is to be moderate in everything. He is given neither to erratic behavior or overreactions. Moderation is a mark of stability. Prudence means sound judgment. Those who shepherd God's people need not only good hearts but good heads as well.

The next quality has been translated "respectable or gentlemanly." But the Greek word *kosmion* would better be translated "orderly." An orderly mind and an orderly life speaks well for leadership. The shepherd care and spiritual oversight of others calls for this quality. Orderliness, a mark of character, must be an inner quality reflected outwardly.

Family Qualities

The New Testament does not explicitly say that elders must be married men, but twice it says they are to be the husband of one wife. Paul is saying that his family life must be of the highest order. The domestic life of a spiritual leader is especially important in today's church. The family suffers attack from every side. The social situation in which modern Christians find themselves is not conducive to healthy family life. The faulty presuppositions of many professionals in the behavior sciences have led them to advocate alternatives to family life. The attack seems to center on the institution of marriage. One absolute of the Christian system an elder is called on to defend and to teach is the sanctity of marriage and the home. A solid marriage and an exemplary home life is a strong asset for an elder. His home as well as his ministry must demonstrate the biblical perception of the family.

The way a man superintends his own home will be reflected in the way he superintends the church as an elder. Can he manage with dignity and love his own household? Are his children in subjection? Have they been instructed in the faith and does their behavior reflect Christian influence? The first test of the elder's ability to "rule" is the domestic test.

Paul details in Titus 1:6 the extent of Christian influence expected in the children of elders. They are to be believers. Their conduct is to be above reproach. They are to have learned the value of obedience. The godly leadership of the husband and father in the home is the key to establishing the children of that home.

A congregation should carefully choose its elders on the basis of their home life.

Leadership Qualities

The lay-elder has the responsibility of assisting the pastor-elder in the spiritual oversight of the believers. This kind of leadership calls for certain abilities on the part of those who undertake it. Paul instructed the church to consider men who were "able to teach" for this position (1 Tim. 3:2). Teaching is essential if the community of believers is to grow. Skill in teaching may come to some as a spiritual gift while others will develop the capability by diligent work and study.

Paul says that elders are also to be able to exhort (Titus 1:9). Exhortation is the art of encouraging believers to put into action what they have learned from teaching. Teaching without exhortation is fruitless; exhortation is the perfect compliment of teaching.

The elder must also be able to refute false doctrines (Titus

1:9), for he has an obligation to guard the flock. The church today is as vulnerable to heresy as was the first century church. The constant vigilance of its leadership is her best defense against the subtle invasion of false doctrine.

The oversight of the church requires its spiritual leaders not only to be knowledgable but able to teach what they know to the people of God.

Social Qualities

The church in addition to being a spiritual sanctuary and a supernatural community is a social institution. The assembly is not isolated from the total community. Its visibility in that community has a bearing on its leadership. Church leaders cannot be oblivious to the social dimension surrounding the church.

An elder is to be hospitable. He should love people and enjoy being with them in a social situation. The elder's home should reflect a wholesome atmosphere. It should be a place where either saint or sinner would feel warmth of love and the riches of Christian hospitality.

An elder is to "live what is good" (Titus 1:8). The ability to love life and promote good commends a man to the whole community. The elder should be a leader who has learned the good things and promotes them in the culture of his community. He is positive in his display of righteousness.

Another important social quality for an elder is his general reputation in the community. If a man is of good reputation outside the church, it means he has learned to glorify God in all his relationships both inside the church and outside the church. If a man is odious in the eyes of the community, he cannot be a leader in the church, at least until a behavior change has corrected this view of his reputation.

Spiritual Qualities

Paul calls for an elder to be above reproach as a servant of God (Titus 1:7). Elders are to be blameless because they are more than commissioned officers of the organized church. They are stewards of God and must ultimately answer to Him. The serious business of answering to God requires the elder to walk in all the spiritual light he possesses.

Being God's steward implies a managerial responsibility to God. One is accountable for the right use of God-given resources. An elder should have settled the money question in his own life. His lifestyle should manifest a commitment to the work of Christ that takes precedence over the materialism of today's society. Lay-elders and pastor-elders ought to excell in stewardship, being models in giving to the work of Christ's church. The elder's tithes and offerings should set an example to inspire faithful stewardship by the whole congregation.

The characteristics of a holy walk and faithful stewardship should be accompanied by fervent worship. Paul urged Titus to consider "devout" men to oversee the flock. The Greek word means pious, one who is inclined to be very devout in his worship of Christ. Intense spiritual hunger in the leadership promotes strong spiritual desire in the rest of the assembly.

Are elders super-saints? Could anyone actually meet the standard for this position in the church? The answers to these and other questions about the qualifications for eldership are found in the scriptures themselves. Elders are not perfect nor are they super-saints. But an elder should be a normal Christian. The standard for normalcy is not arrived at by taking an average of the quality of life in the church. The normal Christian life is described in the scriptures. The spiritual qualifications of eldership do fall in the range of ordinary people. These qualities compose a committed, growing, vital Christian. The man chosen to be an elder may find himself weak in some qualities and want to remove himself from the eldership. He would do better to trust Christ for the needed strength to firm up those aspects of his spiritual life.

The spirit of the man is more important than age, status, training, or experience. A teachable spirit will make him the man of God that an elder should be.

The image of an elder created by some churches is a man who has arrived spiritually. That is a danger sign. To create a mystique around this group of spiritual leaders which immunes them from weakness and makes all their judgments infallible is a radical departure from the New Testament order. Elders should be mature Christians but they must be growing Christians. They must be willing to take the risks to which a true shepherding ministry will expose them.

No better summary of the qualities of an elder has been formulated than that of T. G. Campbell, a Presbyterian elder in Scotland:

> "The essential qualifications of the elder are that he loves God's Son, God's Book, God's House, God's Day and God's Footstool."[1]

---

[1] T. G. Campbell, *The Work of the Eldership,* John Smith and Sons Ltd., Glasgow, 1917, p. 27.

7

The Scriptural Qualifications of Deacons

The qualifications of a deacon may be drawn from two passages in the New Testament. The establishment of the ministry of deacons as recorded in Acts chapter six provides a partial list of qualifications for this office.

But select from among you, brethren, seven men of good reputation, full of the Spirit and wisdom, whom we may put in charge of this task. (Acts 6:3)

The deacon, like the elder, must be a man with a good reputation not only in the church but in the community as well. The duties of his office call for the highest level of confidence. As a very important lay leader the deacon should have the trust of the membership.

The apostles agreed that the deacons selected from the fellowship should be Spirit-filled men. Though their ministry was largely the administration of material things, Spirit-filled men were essential for the oversight of this task. The work assigned the deacons was an integral part of the church's overall ministry.

No dichotomy exists between the spiritual and the material ministries of the church. The deacons elected to wait tables in the household of faith are as much in need of the fulness of the Holy Spirit as the elders who minister the Word.

The infilling of the Holy Spirit is just as essential for service as He is for holy living. Christians so often experience futility in their efforts at service in most instances because of the absence of anointing for service. The norm for every Christian is to be Spirit-filled.

The third characteristic of good deacons given by the apostles was wisdom. The deacon was assigned to an important task requiring him not only to serve himself but to enlist and oversee others in the accomplishment of the task. The deacons were called upon frequently to make decisions and to deal with the problems of people. The deacon must be wise in the sense that he has developed the skill of applying his knowledge in a given situation. He should be a man of good judgment.

As the church grew and spread beyond Palestine to the Gentiles the office of deacon became more important in the life of the church. When Paul instructed Timothy in matters of church order he advised him to have deacons in the churches. Paul's instructions included a guideline of qualifications to assure spiritual leadership in the office of deacon comparable to the standards for the office of elder.

> *Deacons likewise must be men of dignity, not double-tongued, or addicted to much wine or fond of sordid gain,*
> *but holding to the mystery of the faith with a clear conscience.*
> *And let these also first be tested; then let them serve as deacons if they are beyond reproach. . . .*
> *Let deacons be husbands of only one wife, and good managers of their children and their own households.*
> *For those who have served well as deacons obtain for themselves a high standing and great confidence in the faith that is in Christ Jesus. (1 Tim. 3:8-10, 12-13)*

The similarities as well as the differences of the qualifications of deacons to that of elders are important. Three qualities of a deacon are exactly like the qualities of eldership.

The deacon's home life is very important. He must have a solid marriage that meets scriptural standards. He must also have a well-ordered home. His children should reflect in their conduct the Christian atmosphere of the home. The support of a godly wife is certainly implied in this passage.

With the widespread need to strengthen the family this requisite for leadership should not be taken lightly by any church.

The deacon like the elder is not to be addicted to wine. The collective judgment of our fellowship from its inception until now is that believers should not use any form of alcoholic beverages. Since alcoholism is now the most threatening form of drug abuse in western society the Christian community must refrain all the more from the use of alcoholic beverages. The deacons and the elders must provide a wholesome example by their own abstinence.

The financial practices of a candidate for the office of deacon ought not to be overlooked. The scriptures say that he is not to "be fond of sordid gain." The word *sordid* infers a shameful or dishonest gain. When one's love for money and material things is so overpowering that he is willing to compromise Christian principles to get money he is not qualified for church leadership. The deacon like the elder should be above reproach in financial matters. He should have a Spirit-given capacity to use his possessions as a stewardship for the glory of Christ. The way a man handles money is the key to his whole value system. An officer of the church who has responsibility for an important share of the finances should have a deep commitment to the values set forth in the gospel. He not only has responsibility to account for the fund, but he must by his own attitude toward money lead the church to the sanctified management of its resources.

Paul speaks not only of the characteristics of deacons that are similar to those of the elders, but he adds some characteristics not found in the list for elders. Paul advises Timothy that men of dignity should be selected for the *diaconate*. The image of the deacon should be one that commands respect. A deacon must deal with all kinds and all ages of people in the course of his duties. As a servant of Christ his bearing should enable him to minister to all.

The idea of dignity is somewhat tarnished in modern culture. So many leaders in high places have failed that cynicism has taken over in the populous. The unfortunate result of this situation is the immortalization of the undignified. The church is obligated to counter such fuzzy thinking and reassert the credibility of dignity. It is needed in the home, in the government, and in the church. Holy Spirit-implanted dignity is a quality of Christian character.

The person selected to serve as a deacon should be in control not only of his walk but also of his talk. In this ministry the deacon will be in constant contact with people in their homes, making him aware of problems that should never be discussed outside one's secret prayer closet. Careless talk damages the work and the reputation of fellow believers. It is significant that this quality be singled out and emphasized in the instruction for deacons, and that he be encouraged to strictly adhere to this. It is a quality that should be emulated by elders and by every Christian. It is especially important that deacons avoid a double-tongue (1 Tim. 3:8). The Greek word translated *double-tongue* carries the connotation of talebearing. The seriousness of this sin can be more readily understood by comparing Proverbs 11:13 with 1 Timothy 3:8:

> *He who goes about as a talebearer reveals secrets, but he who is trustworthy conceals a matter. (Prov. 11:13)*
> *Deacons likewise must be men of dignity, not double-tongued, or addicted to much wine or fond of sordid gain. (1 Tim. 3:8)*

The control of the tongue is a necessity to the deacon's ministry of compassion and understanding. Only the trustworthy can visit from house to house and enjoy the high privilege of such direct exposure to the weaknesses and faults of the saints. The deacon, and for that matter any leader, can minister only to those who trust him.

The office of deacon requires not only qualities of Christian character; it also requires a deep knowledge of the things of God. Paul says,

> *But holding to the mystery of faith with a clear conscience. (1 Tim. 3:9)*

The mystery of faith speaks of an objective faith, the content of faith. These servants of the church must have more than an ordinary understanding of that body of truth which constitutes the gospel. Deacons should be men who know and love the Word of God. The great doctrines of the Bible are their spiritual sustenance. Deacons are to minister truth with compassion.

This office, like that of the elder, is not for the novice; it requires maturity. Paul instructed Timothy that deacons were to be "tested."

And let these also first be tested; then let them serve as deacons if they are beyond reproach. (1 Tim. 3:10)

Paul's use of the present imperative suggests that the testing of the man should be over a period of time. Some have erroneously concluded that deacons should have a probation period after their election to office. Paul is not suggesting a probation; he is calling for care in the selection of the deacons. Only those who have proven themselves should be considered for the office. R. C. H. Lenski, a Lutheran scholar, supports this position by calling attention to the kind of men selected in Acts six for the *diaconate*. They were tried and proven men, selected from the very best to serve as deacons.

The office of deacon should never be used as a ploy to entice some inactive member into ministry. The deacons are to come from those already active in ministry.

For those who have served well as deacons obtain for themselves a high standing and great confidence in the faith that is in Christ Jesus. (1 Tim. 3:13)

A distinction must be made in this verse between the technical and non-technical use of the word *deacon*. Paul is saying that those selected for the office of deacon should be men who have already served the church well by their unofficial ministry. Faithful service is the most likely way for a promising leader to come to the attention of his brethren. The New International Version seems a better translation of this verse.

Those who have served well gain an excellent standing and great assurance in their faith in Christ Jesus. (1 Tim. 3:13—NIV)

The practice of translating the participle *oi diakonasantes* as the work of a deacon comes from the Episcopal approach to the office of deacon. They follow Catholic tradition which looked upon the *diaconate* as a step in the ranks of the clergy: Men are first ordained deacons and then priests and then bishops. While it is true both from scripture and tradition that some deacons entered the ministry or became elders the Episcopal system can hardly be justified either from this scripture or the church's experience.

Paul is here discussing the qualifications of a good deacon. Paul's concern is that the church select men who have already proven themselves in fruitful ministry. The apostle hastens to explain that active laymen are acquiring a good standing and great boldness in their faith. Spiritual growth for them is the by-product of dedicated ministry.

Deaconesses

No consideration of this passage would be complete without a careful interpretation of 1 Timothy 3:11:

Women must likewise be dignified, not malicious gossips, but temperate, faithful in all things.

The use of *women* rather then *wives* indicates that among those serving in the church's ministry of compassion were women or deaconesses. While the New Testament does not mention an office of deaconess, this verse along with Romans 16:1 and 1 Timothy 5:9-10 indicate that women had a definite ministry in the early church.

Four qualifications are given for those women who serve the church as deaconesses. They are essentially the same qualifications as those required of deacons.

Among the women who ministered were the widows. Paul's instructions to Timothy suggest a category of widows enrolled by the church and supported by the church.

Let a widow be put on the list only if she is not less than sixty years old, having been the wife of one man,
having a reputation for good works; and if she has brought up children, if she has shown hospitality to strangers, if she has washed the saints' feet, if she has assisted those in distress, and if she has devoted herself to every good work. (1 Tim. 5:9-10)

The regulations called for women sixty years of age or older with a record of godly deportment. They no doubt were given opportunities of ministry among the saints such as prayer, teaching younger women, and probably as strength permitted ministry to the sick and suffering. References to their work may be found in writings of the Church Fathers.

H. P. Tiddon, Anglican scholar, suggests that women were admitted to the order of widows on the basis of past active service for Christ. Since advanced age prevented the continuation of that same level of active ministry, the widows gave themselves to devotional ministry rather than the practice of philanthropy.[1]

Sixty does not seem to be an advanced age in modern terms, but considering the shorter life expectancy in the first century, a person reaching sixty years of age was considered very elderly. However, at least one ancient source, the Theodosian Code, sets sixty as the age for deaconesses. The council of Chalcedon set forty as the minimum age of a deaconess.[2]

It cannot be established that the church supported widows from the days of the apostles. They were considered deaconesses, but they did constitute a work force of devoted women essential to the church's total ministry. During the post-Apostolic age the order of widows was gradually absorbed by the order of deaconesses.

Kittle's *Theological Dictionary of the New Testament* suggests that the instruction given the older women in Titus 2:3-5 may provide some insight into the nature of the ministry carried on by widows.[3]

Paul says to Titus:

Older women likewise are to be reverent in their behavior, not malicious gossips, nor enslaved to much wine, teaching what is good,

that they may encourage the young women to love their husbands, to love their children,

to be sensible, pure, workers at home, kind, being subject to their own husbands, that the word of God may not be dishonored. (Titus 2:3-5)

These mature, godly women had a responsibility of pastoral care to the young wives of the congregation. The elders and deacons of the primitive church recognized the role of women in Christian service and provided legitimate outlets of ministry for them.

Phoebe, of Cenchrea, was a business woman who traveled as far as Rome in the course of her activities. In her home church she served as a deaconess and by her faithful ministry won the commendation of the apostle Paul.

The pastoral epistles provide the divine standard for church order. The Holy Spirit gave Paul for the church a basic principal to be followed in selecting leaders and workers. They were all required to be spiritually minded and above reproach in their walk before men.

---

[1] H. P. Liddon, *Explanatory Analysis of St. Paul's First Epistle to Timothy.* Klock and Klock: Minneapolis, reprint 1978, p. 56.

[2] Ibid., p. 56.

[3] Gerhard Kittel, Gerhard Friedrich, *Theological Dictionary of the New Testament,* Vol. IX, Wm. B. Eerdmans; Grand Rapids, 1978 edition, pp. 456, 457.

8

The Ministry of the Lay-Elders

The lay-elder is a member of the local church leadership team, working in a Spirit-directed community. The eldership is not a show room for individualism but an opportunity to coordinate with the whole body the Spirit-imparted gift or gifts of ministry. Lay-elders have a large and diversified range of work. A number of leaders with differing gifts can be involved.

The lay eldership is the pastor-elder's strongest support. They are his immediate helpers in the pastoral task of caring for the church. While the work of elders touches all the ministries of the church the focus of the eldership is upon the spiritual ministries. Every church should have a job description which details the functions assigned the lay-elders. The pastor's imput in drafting this document is critical, for he is the supervisor of the elders since their activities relates to his work. The lay-elders, more than any other members in the assembly, assist the pastor or pastors.

Most of the functions of the eldership fall within the circle of pastoral care. The pastor must know that the elders are committed and prepared for the kinds of spiritual duties they are expected to carry out. It is for this reason the scriptural qualifications for lay-elders are as high as those of the pastor-elder.

The best overview of pastoral care found in scripture is Paul's address to the Ephesian elders.

> *Be on guard for yourselves and for all the flock, among which the Holy Spirit has made you overseers, to shepherd the church of God which He purchased with His own blood. (Acts 20:28)*

The writer to the Hebrews particularizes the pastoral role.

Obey your leaders, and submit to them; for they keep watch over your souls, as those who will give an account. Let them do this with joy and not with grief, for this would be unprofitable for you. (Heb. 13:17)

The shepherding of God's people is first of all the duty of the pastor and secondly the duty of the lay-elders. For the sake of order the pastor takes the leadership in assigning and directing the lay-elders in their work. To maintain unity and efficiency their work must be coordinated.

The Church-Membership Committee

The constitution delegates to the lay-elders the responsibility of the church membership roll, one of the most important jobs in the church. The quality and credibility of the entire congregation is dependent on the state of its membership. The church contends for a born-again membership, and the continuation of that scriptural stand is the obligation of the pastor and the elders. Church membership is sacred in that it demonstrates the believers' identity with the local church. It is a testimony to his commitment. The discipleship of a new believer is not complete until that believer has been baptized and has become a functioning member of the local church.

The membership committee has the responsibility of certifying new members. The lay-elders (and in most churches the pastor or a member of the pastoral staff) interview applicants for membership. The purpose of this interview is to determine if the applicant has a sound testimony of salvation, if he is living a consistent Christian life, and if he understands the obligations of church membership.

Applicants for membership should have completed a course of study for new members prior to their appearance before the elders. It is also a good procedure for the believer to have followed the Lord in water baptism before the interview with the membership committee.

The elders need keen insight for this ministry. They must lovingly deal with the applicant to learn of his readiness for church membership. Care must be taken with new Christians

70

not to expect the same level of maturity found in older Christians. Church membership should not be withheld from a child of God because he has not yet reached his spiritual potential. Becoming a functioning and responsible member of the body may be the best stimulus for his spiritual growth.

A good membership preparation class usually weeds out the people that are not yet ready for membership. The pastor or a lay-elder should be teaching such a class for membership every quarter. If the teacher discerns that a member of the class is not ready for an interview with the membership committee, one of the elders should begin counseling this individual to better learn his spiritual condition and how to correct it.

The final step in the procedure of church membership takes place after attendance at the class for new members and a successful interview with the elders. The applicant is publicly received into the church. The pastor has in his manual a service form for receiving members or he may develop his own ritual. It is appropriate for the elders to stand beside the pastor at this service and extend the right hand of fellowship to the new members at the conclusion of the prayer of dedication.

The elders are responsible to keep the membership roll current. There is no reason for a church to keep on its records the names of people who are deceased, or who have left the community, or who have joined other churches. At every annual meeting an up-to-date list of active members should be posted. The church by-laws may outline the categories of membership, active, inactive, honorary, junior, etc. Each category should be kept current and made a part of the official record of each annual meeting.

The Ministry of Healing

Among the most sacred duties performed by the elders is that of anointing the sick for healing. The apostle James, inspired by the Holy Spirit, gave this ministry to the eldership for as long as the church is on earth.

Is anyone among you sick? Let him call for the elders of the church, and let them pray over him, anointing him with oil in

71

the name of the Lord;

and the prayer offered in faith will restore the one who is sick, and the Lord will raise him up, and if he has committed sins, they will be forgiven him.

Therefore, confess your sins to one another, and pray for one another, so that you may be healed. The effective prayer of a righteous man can accomplish much. (James 5:14-16)

The ministry of healing will be guarded from abuse if the church abides by the instructions of James. The design of this procedure is to give Christ the glory as the true healer. Prayer by a plurality of elders prevents any one individual being identified as the healer. The prayer of faith may be given to any one of the elders, and only God can know which one.

The eldership must devote time and special seasons of prayer to the proper preparation for the ministry of healing. Without diligent prayer this ministry will fail. The scriptures should be studied to provide a basis of faith through the Bibical promises of healing.

Since the anointing of the sick may take place in a member's home or in his hospital room, the elders will need to have free time for this ministry. It is a good policy for each church to have public anointing and prayer for the sick at regular intervals. Perhaps one prayer meeting night a month or at the communion service opportunity could be given for anointing.

The elders should be familiar with the procedures for an anointing service. Whether the ceremony is in a home or at a church service has bearing on the manner in which it is conducted. The pastor should arrange the order of the service in advance. Begin with prayer followed by reading James 5:13-16 and other key passages as an encouragement to faith. If the anointing is done in a public service, a sermon on this doctrine would be appropriate. In a private anointing service some instruction should be given the individual seeking to be healed. After instruction and prayer by one of the elders, the pastor or an elder will place a small amount of oil on the forehead of the person for which the prayer is offered. As his finger touches the forehead he will say, ''My brother (or sister), I anoint you in the name of the Father, and of the Son, and of the Holy Spirit.'' Then the pastor and the elders should lay their hands on the individual while a second prayer is offered.

It would be helpful if in each congregation an elder could be delegated to form and oversee prayer groups to intercede for the ministry of healing.

The Ministry of Counseling

Many modern pastors are draining their strength and dulling their creativity by carrying too large a counseling load. The great number of disturbed people both inside the church and outside the church make the ministry of counseling an obligation. If this need is to be met, others must become involved. The pastor must select from the church's lay leadership people whose gifts make them competent to counsel.

The techniques of counseling are too often drawn entirely from the theories of the behavioral sciences. Christian counseling is based on the Bible. It is the patient, Spirit-directed counsel of one who has been gifted by the Holy Spirit. Quickened insight and sensitivity are needed. The total leadership of the church will make the decisions as to the philosophy of counseling they will endorse. The next step is to train some elders to assist the pastor with this heavy responsibility. The pastor will probably want to teach a course for these elders relating to the principles and methods of counseling. He will then work with them until they are ready to assume assignments on their own.

Discipline

Among some church bodies the discipline of members is relegated to antiquity, but among Bible-believing churches this procedure is still considered relevant. If the church is to shine like a city set on a hill, its members must demonstrate godliness in their daily lives and practices. No believer is sinless or faultless, but those who take God's Word seriously regulate their lives by their knowledge of the divine standards for conduct. When a member conducts himself in such a manner that would bring disgrace on the church it is the duty of the leadership to take disciplinary action. It is generally agreed that immorality, heresy in doctrine, dishonesty in business practices, and rebellion against constituted authority are matters for discipline.

The board of elders are often asked by the church to be the committee on discipline. The elders as the membership committee are best equipped for this function.

A careful examination of the scripture passages dealing with discipline will help each elder to see the necessity and the divine authority for discipline. The regulations of the denomination will also be helpful in preparing the eldership for this ministry. Discipline should be undertaken with humility of spirit. The overriding concern in the disciplinary procedure is the total spiritual recovery of the person being disciplined.

> *Brethren, even if a man is caught in any trespass, you who are spiritual, restore such a one in a spirit of gentleness; looking to yourselves, lest you too be tempted. (Gal. 6:1)*

Visitation

The shepherd care of a congregation requires house-to-house visitation of the membership. The purpose of such visitation is not social but spiritual. If the full responsibility for this work is placed on the pastor and/or his assistants, it probably will not be completed. There are not hours enough in the day, or days enough in the week for one pastor to shepherd his entire congregation with the kind of care they need.

The task of pastoral care must be distributed within the total church labor force. The lay-elders are to share the pastoral visitation of members. A shepherd-elder plan has been used since the Reformation among the Christian Reformed Churches to provide adequate home visitation. With this plan the congregation is divided into zones and a lay-elder is appointed to service each zone. It is the shepherd-elder's responsibility to visit each home in his zone once a quarter and to report to the pastor the results of that visit. The success of the shepherd-elder plan is dependent on a good reporting system. The pastor may provide forms for writing out the report. Verbal consultation on problem areas are important. If the lay-elder discovers a home needs a visit from the pastor, he makes the pastor aware of that need.

Some ground rules should be followed in visiting homes, to insure against making just social calls. During each visit the elder should read the scripture, have prayer, and discuss any spiritual needs the family may have. Every effort should be made to visit when the whole family is present. Home visitation should contribute to the strengthening of the family. The elder may be tempted to minister only to the adult members of the family. The elder must develop the art of communicating with children and young people if he is to succeed in family visitation.

Regular home visits will promote the general unity of the assembly and encourage spiritual growth. The regularity of the program will teach the families of the church that they need not wait until a crisis arises to receive spiritual support and consultation from the church.

The elder who does home visitation should be well enough informed about the church to answer questions. He should be well taught in doctrine and able to instruct the family.

The lay-elder must resist any effort to play his leadership role against that of the pastor, for they are coworkers. By training the lay-elder to share the work of home visitation the pastor is enlarging the church's scope of ministry and enriching it by the use of several of God's gifted servants from the laity.

The involvement of lay-elders makes it possible for every church family to get the attention from the leadership that it should have. Such a visitation program will increase church attendance, improve stewardship and increase the number of homes where family altar is consistently conducted by the family head.

Evangelism

The elders not only assist the pastor with the shepherd care of the congregation but they share his concern for the lost. The evangelization of the community is a high priority for any evangelical church. The pastor cannot be the only soul winner in the leadership if this task is to be accomplished. All church leaders should participate in the evangelistic outreach of the fellowship.

A primary need in most churches is a plan to train the people gifted in evangelism. The time and supervision required to train

75

these workers is again more than the pastor alone can handle. The elders provide the logical resource persons for expanding the evangelism program. The Biblical content of personal evangelism must be taught the elders. Having a working knowledge of the subject, they need the firsthand experience of going house-to-house or some other form of evangelistic approach. The pastor must show the elders how he wins people to Christ.

Some of the elders who become burdened for this ministry will make ideal trainers and overseers of the church's evangelism teams. Elders can teach the soul-winners courses. Some can be assigned to train workers by direct example. Someone needs to be appointed to oversee the program by gathering reports, encouraging workers, making them realize that there is accountability in the ministry they have undertaken for Christ.

The home Bible study is one of the most effective means of soul winning today. Those attending a home Bible study invite their unconverted friends who show an interest in the Scriptures to attend. The class leader brings a simple Bible lesson which points up the plan of salvation. This program should be more widely used if lay people were recruited to minister in evangelistic Bible studies. The board of elders may have in their ranks a man with the gifts needed to oversee the Bible study ministry. An elder could train other laymen to teach the classes. He would then oversee the total program by locating homes for classes. By arranging follow-up for new converts Bible classes would then have a continuously growing outreach.

The Lord's Supper

No greater honor is given an elder than that of assisting the pastor in the serving of the Lord's Supper. Communion is the church's family gathering. The seating of the pastor and elders about the table symbolizes the whole church family. Christ has invited the saints to His banquet of love, a high and holy time of worship. The Supper is a time of mutual sharing. The breaking of the bread often inspires new faith as hearts well up in praise and thanksgiving at the contemplation of Calvary. It's a grand celebration of the death and resurrection of the Lord Jesus Christ. The communion meal is a prophecy of His coming again and the better table to be spread in His kingdom. To be a servant at Christ's table is a great honor. It should never be looked upon as a mere ritual, nor should the children of God ever tire of this sacred gathering.

The lay-elders not only help serve the elements but they minister in prayer and in the reading of the Word of God. On some occasions they may bring exhortations to the congregation. The deep involvement of the lay-elders in this ordinance underscores the Protestant understanding of this family feast of love.

Other Shepherd Responsibilities

The development of the ministries of lay-elders certainly includes teaching. Since every church needs a total training program to continuously prepare workers for every kind of ministry the elders provide a corps of teacher trainers for this need. Elders should be able to teach others so well that they in turn will teach others.

Some elders will function as lay preachers. They may never become pastors, but will use their preaching ability wherever it is needed. The pastor should encourage and train any elders which manifest this ability. Such lay preachers can be invaluable in planting new churches mothered by the congregation. Some become so effective they will take the pulpit ministry while the pastor is on vacation. An elder with a gift of evangelistic preaching may hold successful evangelistic campaigns. There is always a need for preachers for jail ministry, rescue missions, men's meetings and many other possibilities. More attention should be given the potential for preaching by lay-elders.

The follow-up of new believers is another area for the ministry of lay-elders. Not everyone is especially able to deal with new-born Christians. The elders who show aptitude for this work should be trained to oversee the ministry of follow-up.

Every church needs adequate altar workers to counsel with seekers who come forward during a public invitation. The elders should organize this aspect of evangelism. They may train lay altar workers, select and provide literature for this work and oversee the altar services.

This chapter does not begin to exhaust the possibilities of lay-elder ministry. As churches grow their need for leadership grows. The eldership keeps finding new and creative ways to support leadership of their pastor and to promote the involvement of the laity in the service of Christ.

9

The Ministry of the Deacons

The word *minister* is common to all who serve Christ in His church. It occurs some one hundred times in the New Testament referring both to the service of the clergy and the laity. The apostle Paul spoke of himself as a minister in Colossians 1:23. In Ephesians 4:12 the work of the ministry means the Christian service of every member of the body of Christ. The Lord Jesus Christ is called a "minister." Against such a broad understanding of ministry it is necessary to place the technical concept of ministry as it relates to deacons and to their female counterparts, the deaconesses.

The same Greek word translated minister is also translated deacon. Deacon is an English transliteration of the Greek word. The deacon is a special kind of minister characterized by compassion and concern for the needs of others. The nature of his office is an index to his work. The first seven deacons were selected at the direction of the apostles to increase the work force of the Jerusalem church. The deacons were to assume leadership in the work for which their gifts fitted them and by so doing would release other brethren whose gifts were prayer and the ministry of the Word.

The modern deacon has just as important a role as did the ancient deacons. With the complexity of society and the sophistication of the church more servants than ever are needed to do the work. Every church needs well-qualified deacons.

The Leadership Role of the Deacon

The office of deacon is a position of leadership. The deacon does not personally perform all the ministries assigned the deacon board. As a leader he recruits and trains helpers so the work force is large enough to carry out its responsibilities. In far too many churches the deacon does all the work relating to the material aspects of the church. The *diaconate* can enlarge its ministry by involving other lay people in the work. The board of deacons should determine those deacons with the gifts to enlist others and teach them the work. One deacon could be delegated to such a ministry. Other deacons may have gifts of evangelism, or of showing mercy, or of giving. All of these abilities enhance the work of the deacon board.

Each church will want to write its own job description for deacons listing the areas the leadership has agreed should be their function. That guideline should include at least some of the tasks discussed in this chapter. The local church, because of its circumstances, may create other functions for the deacons.

The Distribution of Benevolences

Traditionally, deacons have been assigned to administer the benevolences of the church. Jesus said, "The poor you have always with you." In affluent modern nations there are still the poor. The poor among the saints should be the first concern of the church. The church must think of the poor in the non-Christian community and seek to minister to them. True social concern born of the love of God is the paramount task of the deacon.

Churches located in large metropolitan areas may be surrounded by poverty. The church may be in a changing neighborhood with two or more ethnic communities moving toward control. Because of a poorly conceived deaconship the opportunities to minister in such a community are overlooked. The deacons can build bridges to the community at large. Some congregations have been blessed by establishing "head-start" classes for ethnic children. Family clinics to instruct people in the productive use of their money would be a help. If language is a problem, provide translators and services for people with little or no knowledge of English. Help them find jobs, fill out alien papers and offer classes to teach them English. Practical ministries of this kind in the poor community will open doors for the gospel.

It is not unusual for families within the church to suffer disasters that leave them destitute. The deacons should have at their disposal money that can be used to relieve the needs of the suffering. Many congregations follow the practice of taking a free-will offering for the deacons' fund at each communion service. Some funds should probably be budgeted for the deacons fund. A loss of job, extended illness, fires, floods, earthquakes and many other conditions come upon both Christian and the non-Christian. The credibility of the church's compassion is established as much by what it does for its own as by what it does for the non-church people.

The Senior Citizen

The twentieth century church has an exciting opportunity of ministry to the elderly. There are more people of retirement age than ever before in our culture. The needs of this group are not always financial. Elderly people need personal attention. Provision should be made for them to participate in group activity. A sizable work force should be assigned to this ministry. Some of the deacons as well as members of the congregation should give this ministry their attention.

Elderly people who are shut-in and unable to attend church should not be left out of the life and activity of the church. Deacons could visit them on a regular basis and teach them the Sunday school lesson. Every church needs a home department for these people in its Sunday school. When the line of communications are kept open these people can make a contribution to the church. Some might be able from their wheel chair or bed to use a telephone. A part of the church's telephone prayer chain could be given them to make contacts when special prayer requests are being circulated. Find something meaningful for them to do. They should be given a church bulletin each week and a set of offering envelopes. In one church pastored by the author two of the biggest contributors to foreign missions were shut-ins past seventy years of age. With a little effort the home department could be ministering to a hundred people. They and their families would know that the church cares.

Ministry to the Sick

The ministry of the deacons to the sick is an ancient tradition.

81

While the elders are delegated to the ministry of healing, the deacons have the practical care of the sick. How helpful to a family with the mother hospitalized to have the evening meal prepared and brought to the home. What a relief to the husband and father to have a baby sitting service for his pre-school age children while he visits the hospital. What wife would not be comforted by the fact that the deacons cared for the lawn while her husband was hospitalized or perhaps they finished an incompleted paint job. The ministry of compassion to the sick and their families must go beyond a card and some flowers. Changing off nights with a weary spouse at the bedside of a seriously sick husband or wife would help so much to lift their load of care.

Hospitality

The *diaconate* has a ministry of hospitality. The need for entertaining fellow Christians when they traveled was necessary in the ancient church. Public inns and taverns were not available to Christians so the saints opened their homes for this purpose. Modern believers do not have this problem. Motels and hotels are everywhere, with food service and just about any service needed by the traveler. But though the culture has changed, the need for hospitality has not changed. What an exciting ministry a deacon and his family could enjoy by opening their home to overseas missionaries arriving at an airport near their location. Providing overnight lodging, meals, and transportation for the missionary family would be a wonderful expression of the love of Christ in terms of true hospitality.

What about the many new families that visit the church in the course of a month. Each of them could be invited to a home for Sunday dinner. This kind of hospitality would demonstrate the real concern of the church for people and not just statistics.

The deacons might be assigned to oversee the ushers since ushering is a form of hospitality. The initial impression of visitors to the church are often formed by the conduct of the ushers. While the deacons probably cannot assume this task themselves because of their work load, they could be in charge of recruiting, training and overseeing the ushers.

The deacons, deaconesses, and their families are not personally responsible to care for all of the hospitality needs of the church. They should set a good example by their own participation in this ministry, but they must unite all the members in doing the work of entertaining strangers.

The Deacons and the Ordinances

The elders are usually in charge of the spiritual ministries of the church and assist the pastor with the preparation of candidates for baptism and in the distribution of the Lord's Supper. Traditionally the deacons have also related to both of these ordinances. The provision and maintenance of the equipment necessary for baptism is often the work of the deacons. Deaconesses are usually responsible for maintaining and laundering the baptismal robes. The deacons can be enlisted to assist the men at the baptismal service while the deaconesses assist the women. It is helpful to have one of the deacons standing by the baptistry or standing by the pastor in the baptistry to assist him in the event of any difficulty. Good organization and proper planning can make the mechanics of the service something worthy of its high spiritual meaning.

Another humble but beautiful service for deacons and deaconesses is the care of the communion ware. Maintaining a fresh supply of unleavened bread and the grape juice is essential. Washing and storing the communion ware after each service and laundering the linens can be done for the glory of God. A practical system for this responsibility is to assign a deacon and his wife to care for the communion preparation each quarter of the year. One of the deacons should be put in charge of instructing the communion custodians as to their responsibility and the proper procedure. Data should be given them as to the number of portions to prepare. How many reserve portions should there be for unexpected guests or a larger than usual attendance of members. They should also be instructed as to setting the table. The deacon in charge of communion custodians should confer regularly with the pastor as to any necessary change in procedure.

In some churches the elders on a regular basis ask the deacons to assist them in the distribution of the elements at the communion service. It is also helpful for deacons to assist the pastor and the elders in serving communion to the shut-ins and the sick.

Stewardship

The finances of the local church are a part of the broad concerns of the deacons. The distribution of the benevolences of the church is only the beginning of their concern with finances. The deacon board is the ideal agency of the local church structure to promote stewardship. The average evangelical church fails to train its membership in the Christ-like use of their money. The proper management of money and material resources is a Christian's duty. Stewardship, a necessary discipline for the godly, is a form of service to Christ. Either the believer learns to control his money or his money will control him.

Christians need basic instructions about the stewardship of time, talents, possessions, and money. If every Christian were to obey the Spirit in this regard there would be no financial lack in the ministries of the church. Out of the abundance flows money to finance the overseas outreach and all the supporting institutions at home. The deacons should be knowledgable in what the Bible teaches on this subject, and conducting classes for the membership. They should distribute sound literature on tithing and all forms of giving. A strong *diaconate* might comprise the finance committee for the congregation.

The deacons may discover some of their members are able to give wise counsel regarding the Christian use of money. Families with extremely difficult financial problems could be counseled by understanding members of the deacon board. Such assistance can revolutionize a family. The right use of their money would not only give them the joy of sharing with Christ but it would greatly improve their living conditions.

Ministry to Special Community Needs

The jails, prisons, and other corrective institutions should not be overlooked by the local church in its compassionate outreach to the community. In most communities it is possible for responsible church representatives to minister to the prisons.

Regular services, Bible classes, and literature brings light and blessing within the bleak walls of these institutions. The deacons provide the logical leadership for such a program. Some deacons may have a burden for this work and show evidence that the Holy Spirit has gifted them to reach the hearts of prisoners. From this leadership a team may be selected to cover the penal institutions in the area.

The deacons' ministry goes beyond contact with the prisoners. The families of the prisoners have great needs which are often neglected by both the community and the church. The deacons and the deaconesses will find it most rewarding to minister to prisoners and their families.

The Deacons and Minorities or Ethnics

The influx of new immigrants and refugees plus the black population and aboriginals make the United States and Canada a veritable mosaic of diverse people. The life of the church in today's world is deeply touched by the realities of such pluralism. The rate of neighborhood change is sometimes so rapid as to leave a congregation in ruin and frustration. Some of this could be avoided if the church would keep constant surveilance of its community and react in love to the changes that take place. When new people come into a neighborhood whose language, race, and culture are different from the old residents, some serious effort to build bridges to these new people must come from the church. It should be remembered that the first deacons were appointed in response to tension between two different culture groups, the Hellenistic Jews and the Aramaic-speaking Jews. Modern deacons are called to deal with the same tensions. If the community requires it, some deacons should be assigned to the task of communicating the love of Christ to new neighbors.

In 1970, the Home Missions Board of the Christian Reformed Church called a conference of selected pastors and laymen to discuss the church's mission in today's world. A book containing the papers of that conference was published with the title, *Who in the World?* It speaks in everyday language about the church's ministry to the non-Christian community. It consistently takes the reader back to the New Testament church to demonstrate the fact that the early church had discovered the forms and methods of effective ministry in the world. The *diaconate* is singled out as an example of a New Testament office that is relevant for now.

"The *diaconate*, then, is the organizational way of accepting from Jesus His sign of the towel, the symbol of servanthood. But two things have to be remembered here: First, the whole church is a *diaconate*. For practical reasons, some of the servant's task is done by deacons. But Jesus' whole life was spent in service, and this is what He asks of all who follow Him. *Diaconate* spells out the whole character, the full spirit, and the great purpose of the church's mission in the world. The body of Christ is not a loose body of separated functions. The whole body is involved in the service. And the official deacons have the right to tap the talents and resources of every member. For we are all limbs of one body."[1]

Never in the long history of the church has the office of deacon been so necessary. Never has it had such broad opportunities of ministry. The modern deacon is a model of servanthood to the congregation. He is a leader in that he discovers and motivates into action the latent abilities in the congregation. The deacon is the church's best liason to the non-Christian community.

---

[1] Clifford Christians, Earl Schipper, Wesley Smeder, *Who in the World?*, William B. Eerdmans Publishing Co., Grand Rapids, 1972, p. 134.

10

Spiritual Gifts for Elders and Deacons

The New Testament speaks of leaders that are gifted by the Holy Spirit for ministry. The term gift is used to translate the Greek word *charismata. Charismata* is related to the Greek word for grace and speaks of divinely imparted ability to minister. Therefore, this kind of leadership is called *charismatic* leadership in theological treatments of the subject. (This term should not be confused with today's popular use of the term charismatic as it refers to the neo-Pentecostal movement.) Some church renewal writers and some church historians have insisted that the church in its purest days, the days of the apostles, knew only a charismatic leadership. The argument continues that office-bearing positions of leadership became prominent as the charismatic leadership phased out. The difficulty with that position is readily seen upon examining the New Testament record. The office-bearing elders and deacons emerged early in the experience of the church and existed along side the charismatic leadership. In fact, spiritual gifts were necessary to the office-bearing leaders so that no noticeable dichotomy existed between office-bearing leaders and charismatic leaders in the first century church. The leadership of the early church was one as should be the leadership of the modern church. Elders and deacons on occasion exercised the gifts listed in Ephesians 4:11. Elders functioned in pastoral care roles and as teachers. Phillip, one of the deacons of the Jerusalem church, was greatly used of God as an evangelist and a church planter.

The gifts of the Holy Spirit are not religious playthings but rich provisions of His grace for the purpose of ministry. Ministry is synonymous with service. The only proper use of gifts is to glorify Jesus Christ by serving Him. That explains Peter's reference to the exercise of gifts as stewardship (1 Pet. 4:10). Believers must some day in the presence of Christ give an account of their use of the gifts imparted by His Spirit.

To possess a gift is to be responsible for the use and the development of that God-given ability for the glory of Christ and the edification of His church. Peter said,

> *As each one has received a special gift, employ it in serving one another, as good stewards of the manifold grace of God. (1 Pet. 4:10)*

The Stewardship of Gifts

Gifts are designed for ministry. Peter's use of the term *steward* associates the appropriate use of gifts with the role of the servant. Arndt and Gingrich translate the Greek word *kaloi oikonomoi* as

"good administrators of the varied grace of God."[1]

The steward was a manager or administrator usually of his master's property. As a servant he exercised all the ability he could muster to make his master's investment profitable. The investment of Christ in the believer is the ability to minister for the good of others. To waste that gift is a loss to the believer, to others, and to God.

Gifts and Leadership

The gifts are not only related to ministry in the New Testament scriptures, they are also related to leadership in the church. The leader Christ calls He also equips with gifts appropriate to his responsibility. It is remarkable how many of the gifts are by their very nature intended for leadership. This concept is especially obvious in Eph. 4:11-12:

> *And He gave some as apostles, and some as prophets, and some as evangelists, and some as pastors and teachers, for the equipping of the saints for the work of service, to the building up of the body of Christ.*

88

In the above passage Paul names five functions of ministry necessary to the church's welfare. He is more concerned with the people who minister than with their particular gifts. The gifted officers enumerated here are a special gift of Christ to His church.

The apostle Paul evidently saw a close relationship between leadership and gifts. Another passage in his epistles relating to this subject is 1 Cor. 12:28-30:

> *And God has appointed in the church, first apostles, second prophets, third teachers, then miracles, then gifts of healings, helps, administrations, various kinds of tongues.*
>
> *All are not apostles, are they? All are not prophets, are they? All are not teachers, are they? All are not workers of miracles, are they?*
>
> *All do not have gifts of healings, do they? All do not speak with tongues, do they? All do not interpret, do they?*

In listing the divine appointments for leadership the Apostle mixes the offices with the gifts. He moves from talking about persons, apostles, prophets, and teachers to the abstract term *miracles* as though they were related items in a sequence. He meant by that abstract term those who do miracles. The implication of this sequence is that all who have an office have a gift. It is the responsibility of the assembly to select men to office which possess a gift corresponding to that office. The contemporary church tends to select men to office without regard to their gifts. The inevitable result of such an unscriptural procedure is poor leadership contributing to the progressive decline of the church. Effective ministry must be in the power of the Holy Spirit. The leadership of Christ's church is gifted by the Spirit to assure spiritual ministry to the body.

Necessary Credentials for Leadership

The gifts of the Holy Spirit are given to equip leaders for their ministry to the church. Enabling for Christian service is divine. Natural talents, attractive personality, wide experience, and a good education may do much to enrich a person's life, but none of these qualities fit a man to serve Christ. The natural man makes his judgments of character on the outward appearance, but this method will not suffice in the selection of Christian leadership.

The church needs from its leaders sound teaching, wisdom, protection, guidance, direction and good order. The abilities to service these needs come from the Holy Spirit. Pastor-elders, lay-elders, and deacons must have gifts to minister to the body as Christ intends they should. The gifts given to leaders are for the purpose of equipping every believer for service. If gifts are neglected at the leadership level, the possibility of the gifts of all the members coming into use is very unlikely.

Safeguards to the purity and vitality of the church have been built into the divine order of the church administration and ministry. Positions of leadership have their own peculiar kinds of temptation. Pride and the abuse of authority are the most insidious and those which most frequently occur. Honoring the New Testament principle of gifts is one means of overcoming these temptations. Dr. A. B. Simpson grasped this truth in Paul's discussion of the order of gifts.

"The order of spiritual gifts is very instructive and also humiliating. The first mentioned gifts are those of the apostles, prophets and teachers, the spiritual ministries of the church. Next comes the miraculous gifts of healing subordinate to spiritual ministry—important but not preeminent. Thirdly comes the helps, people that just fit in, and by love, fellowship and prayer and often subordinate service, fill up the innumerable places and become the countless links without which all else would be in vain. After these in a lower order, come the governments, the rulers, the people with authority, wisely placed near the bottom to keep them from falling over with the weight of importance. No one can rule another until he has walked in the ranks and learned to keep his head low."[2]

Though the function of administration is fraught with dangers of spiritual pride, lording it over the flock, and self-aggrandizement it is nevertheless essential to the wellbeing of the church. It is so essential that the Holy Spirit distributes gifts for the purpose of effective administration. Mention is made in

1 Cor. 12:30 of the gift of "governments" or as the newer versions put it "administrations." The Greek word *kubernasis* comes from a verb form meaning "to steer." It is a nautical term and could be translated "shipmaster" or "helmsman." It refers to one who steers a ship. Kittle says of this word,

> "The reference can only be to the specific gifts which qualify a Christian to be a helmsman to his congregation, i.e., a true director of its order and therewith of its life."
>
> ". . . No society can exist without some order and directions. It is the grace of God to give gifts which equip for government."[3]

The principles of management have become an important field of study in modern terms. The size and complexity of business, institutions, and government require very competent and sophisticated administration. The New Testament teaches that the expertise to manage the house of God is on an entirely different basis. Divine management is a charisma given by the Holy Spirit to those called to leadership.

The pastor and the elders are under mandate to give order to the life and activities of the church. God has called the pastor in particular to be a helmsman of the ship of Zion, the church. More than one administrator is needed in a congregation. The pastor should have the ability to oversee the work and to coordinate the efforts of all who display this gift. Lay-elders as well as pastors may have the gift of administration. The church is sailing through troubled waters at this point in history and desperately needs men at the helm that lead with certainty and confidence.

The second gift related to church government is found in Romans 12:8:

> *. . . he who leads with diligence . . .*

The Greek word *proistamenos* literally means to be placed in the front of the line. The King James Version translates it "rule." It is the gift of ruling in the sense of leading the congregation. Kittle finds a deeper meaning in the context of this word.

"In most cases *proistami* seems to have the sense 'to lead,' but context shows in each case that one must take into account sense 'to care for . . .' this is explained by the fact that caring was the obligation of leading members of the infant church. . . ."[4]

The gift of leading is also associated with the pastor. The three principle passages dealing with the pastor-elder all use some form of this verb (1 Thess 5:12; I Tim. 3:5; 5:17) indicating that a pastor must be a good leader. He is the example and the teacher of leadership principles to the laymen. The responsibilities of church leadership are so complex and far reaching that a wise pastor will encourage the gift of leadership among the lay elders. Such gifted lay leaders share with the pastor the responsibility of envisioning the church's work and articulating that vision to the congregation.

The Gift of Prophecy

The pastor's primary function is preaching the Word of God. There are spiritual gifts which relate to this important function. Prophecy is one such gift. Ordinarily prophecy is interpreted to mean foretelling future events. It does have that function at times, but most of the prophecy found in scripture is straightforward preaching which applies revealed truth to the current situation of the people of God. Not all preaching is prophecy but it is one kind of preaching needed in every congregation. A lay-elder may also have the gift of prophecy, with unusual insight into the spiritual needs of the congregation. The pastor should cherish and nurture the gift of prophecy wherever he may find it among the lay-elders.

The apostle Paul in his first letter to Timothy makes an interesting statement regarding the gift of prophecy as it relates to the eldership.

Do not neglect the spiritual gift within you, which was bestowed upon you through prophetic utterance with the laying on of hands by the presbytery. (I Tim. 4:14)

Apparently at Timothy's ordination elders were given the insight by the Holy Spirit to identify Timothy's gift for ministry. Paul advises Timothy to develop that gift by diligent study and faithful service.

Pastoral Care

Since both pastors and lay-elders engage in pastoral care the gift of shepherding will equip them for this ministry. The flock of God not only needs oversight but they also need to be fed and guided and guarded. Pastoral care is an art learned from the Chief Shepherd, the Lord Jesus Christ. He imparts through the Holy Spirit the enabling to care for God's people. Pastoral care implies a direct personal ministry to the people of the congregation. To have the insights, skills and patience to shepherd the great diversity of people which make up any one congregation requires divine assistance. Many churches suffer from the lack of pastoral care. If the pastor must carry this whole load in addition to his other required duties, the individual needs of the fellowship will go unattended. The pastor may multiply his ability to do the work of pastoral care by finding and developing among the elders those with gifts for this work.

The Gifts of Healings

Christ gave to His church the ministry of healing. In Christ's name and by His authority the church is commissioned to heal. The prescribed order of the healing ministry is revealed in the scripture. When Christians are sick they are to call the elders of the church. The elders are instructed by the scriptures to anoint the sick with oil and pray over them in the name of Jesus.

Since the elders have been assigned this ministry it is reasonable to believe that the gifts of healings are most frequently distributed among the elders. The Biblical order for a healing service calls for a plurality of elders to participate in anointing and prayer. When the Biblical order is carried out the integrity of the ministry of healing is maintained. Christ is always projected as the Healer. The elders and the whole church should look to Christ as Head over His church to give the eldership the gifts of healings necessary to meet their congregational needs.

Since the deacons of the church are not engaged in oversight

93

and pastoral care their gifts coincide with their ministries. The New Testament suggests a number of gifts that should be exercised by the *diaconate*. The deacons of the church need gifts that fit them for ministries of compassion. They serve the practical needs of the family of God and sometimes the non-Christian community. Peter and Paul both speak of the gift of service. Certainly every deacon and deaconess needs the gift of service and they need the strength which God supplies to perform that service (1 Pet. 4:11). The deacon who devotes his time to ministering in a sick room will need the gift of showing mercy. One man of God spent years in a large city hospital shaving patients, trimming their toe nails and finger nails. This unglamorous ministry opened up doors of blessing and gospel outreach that many a pastor would envy. The gift of the Spirit is always exactly what is needed to do the work, but the gift can function only when the believer has consecrated himself to service.

The Gift of Helps

The same Holy Spirit who gifted men in the time of Moses to work in precious metal and other highly skilled crafts necessary in constructing the tabernacle, gifts deacons today to use tools to serve Christ in the caring of the church's physical properties. The hammer and the saw used in the name of Christ is a ministry. The oversight of the buildings to maintain proper repairs and an attractive appearance is also a ministry unto the Lord. The deacons or other lay leaders called by the body and by the Lord to these ministries have every right to believe that the Holy Spirit will gift them for their labors.

The Gift of Giving

The very nature of the deacon's work would give him a concern for Christian stewardship. The deacon seeks to use the church's resources to help those in need. What better gift might a deacon possess than that of giving. Paul explains the gift of giving should be exercised with liberality (Rom. 12:8). The generosity of the deacons should provide an example for the whole congregation. The consistent giving of leadership encourages every member to honor the Lord by their own faithfulness in giving.

The Gift of Faith

Some gifts are distributed to all the leaders of the church and among these is the gift of faith. It must be understood that faith in this context does not refer to saving faith but rather a working faith. It is the faith to believe that God will work out His plan and provide abundantly for it. Leadership may dream dreams and have visions of outreach and enlargement, but they will never be launched without faith. Most of God's work must be undertaken with inadequate resources and in the face of seemingly unsurmountable obstacles. The success of the project can only be attributed to the fact that God is pleased with the faith of His people. Faith unlocks for the church the invisible supply of resources in the heavenly places. The present affluence of churches in the western world has not removed the need to trust God for His work. The church on the move is the church whose pastor, elders, and deacons seek God's will for the church's ministry and in simple faith believe Him for the resources to accomplish that ministry.

The gifts of the Spirit speak of the continued need of the supernatural in the life of the church. While churches own properties, handle large sums of money, recruit and train people, the church is not just another organization or a business or a corporation. The success of the work of Christ's church has a divine origin. Whatever helpful ideas may be drawn from modern management concepts and other disciplines of learning, they cannot replace the need for the gifts of the Spirit.

---

[1] W. F. Arndt and F. W. Gingrich, *A Greek-English Lexicon of the New Testament and other Early Christian Literature,* University of Chicago, Chicago, 1974 edition, p. 562.

[2] A. B. Simpson, *Christ in the Bible Series: I Corinthians,* Christian Publications, Inc., Harrisburg, Pa., p. 102.

[3] Gerhard Kittle, *Theological Dictionary of The New Testament,* Vol. III, Wm. B. Eerdmans, Grand Rapids, 1978 edition, p. 1036.

[4] Ibid., Vol. VI, p. 701.

11

The Preparation of Elders and Deacons

The equipping of the church officers for ministry after they have been selected and commissioned by the church is largely neglected in modern congregations. Though they be gifted and demonstrate quality Christian living and obvious leadership abilities, the elders and the deacons need training for their tasks.

The pastor-elder does well to devote a part of his time to the training of the church's most important lay leadership. Having taken the elders and deacons through this initial study of their role responsibility and resources he may direct them into further study programs to enrich their ministry. The growing church must be something of a Bible institute teaching and training workers.

Rethinking Priorities

The average layman elected to the eldership or *diaconate* is an active person, perhaps a business or professional man. In many instances his involvement in the community and other organizations take up large segments of his time. If his leadership abilities are well known, a number of para-church groups have probably solicited him to serve on their boards. Family responsibilities claim his time and energies. Hobbies and sports enjoy the remnant of time left from his busy schedule.

When such an active man is elected to serve Christ and His church as an elder or deacon something must change in his schedule of activities. To be an effective elder or a deacon requires time and energy. The responsibilities of these important offices cannot be executed in time left over from an active life. To take these offices seriously calls for a rethinking of one's priorities in light of the call to serve as elder or deacon.

An appraisal of each activity will have to be made to determine its relative value. The activities of lesser importance may have to be dropped to provide the time for study, prayer, and ministry as an elder or a deacon. Consultation with the pastor or a mature lay leader may prove helpful in making this necessary adjustment.

Include the Family

First in the heart and concerns of any church officer should be the best interests and spiritual welfare of his own family. As the priest of his home the family is his first ministry obligation. The work of the church will likely reduce the time available for family activities, but it should not totally replace it. It has already been established that the credibility of a church leader is reflected in a wholesome family life.

The newly elected elder or deacon will find it helpful to call a family conference to discuss his new responsibilities. The wife and children should have a basic understanding of the job and just how important it is to the whole church. Share with them the scriptures describing the office and its responsibilities. As a family, discuss the adjustments that can be made to provide time for ministry. Pray as a family about this ministry. The elder or deacon will find the support of his family a great encouragement.

Start a Self-Study Program

For the elder or deacon who desires a fruitful ministry the initial training course will not be enough. He will want to launch an on-going self-study program that will assure him progressive maturity as an office-bearing leader in the congregation. Self-study programs require self-discipline. The areas of study must be carefully selected and adequate time devoted to the program. Just spending a half hour a day would make it possible to achieve some desirable study goals.

Attractive helps must be given to encourage laymen who perhaps have not studied for years and now find it necessary to recover this discipline in their lives. The newer elders and deacons may not have a personal library of good books. The church should provide a basic collection of study helps. It should also include devotional books, missionary literature, Christian education, evangelism and church growth.

The elder or deacon working with his pastor on a self-study program will need to discover his capacity for study and find the pace of study that is best for him. Starting on a program which is too ambitious will result in discouragement and ultimate abandonment of it. Set realistic goals for yourself. A self-study program to be successful must be a voluntary undertaking. It is a rewarding experience for those who desire to serve Christ with their very best.

Study Doctrine

The elder or deacon after the study of the significance of his own office and its place in the church needs to enlarge his abilities by the study of doctrine. A course in basic Christian doctrine will lay a foundation on which he can build by personal reading and study.

Every lay leader can profit from instruction in the theology and the methods of evangelism. The critical role of elders and deacons in the evangelistic enterprise calls for a knowledge of Biblical evangelism. He must know the field well enough to share it with others and he should be prepared to do personal evangelism. The evangelistic outreach of the congregation requires the mobilization of the potential work force in the congregation. This is not done in most churches because the pastoral and lay leadership do not know how to win souls.

Elders and deacons need to understand the doctrine of the church. The low view of the church so prevalent in the modern scene has resulted in the put down of the church without understanding this blessed and divine institution of our Lord. Each leader needs to be instructed in what the Bible says about the church Christ has established as His visible agent on earth.

The major doctrines of the Christian faith are outlined in the *Statement of Faith* adopted by General Council. As official workers must study this statement and come to understand it as a summary of what the Christian and Missionary Alliance understands the scriptures to teach on these doctrines, so lay leaders need the same process. The *Statement of Faith* does not exhaust the doctrines of the church, but only introduces them in their most rudimentary form. Each article of the statement is worthy of indepth study and further reading on that doctrine.

Historically the Christian and Missionary Alliance has articulated its emphasis on the sufficency of Christ by the term "The Fourfold Gospel." By that is meant Christ our Saviour, Christ our Sanctifier, Christ our Healer, and Christ our Coming King. This arrangement of truth was designed to place special emphasis on areas of doctrine most frequently neglected by the church at large. Lay leaders will want to read the *Fourfold Gospel* by Dr. A. B. Simpson. It is a devotional treatment of these four important aspects of Christology. Continuing study in these doctrinal emphases will equip both elders and deacons to help the congregation adorn the doctrine of Christ.

Bible Study

The overriding concern in an elder's or deacon's self-improvement should be Bible study. It can be assumed that a man selected for this ministry would have regular Bible reading habits and would have learned to feed his own heart on the truth of God's Word. Now he must come to know the Bible better, for his ministry calls for Bible knowledge. In visiting and counseling people he must know the Bible well enough to answer the questions presented by inquirers after truth. He must be able to answer the critics of the gospel as well. He must know the Bible well enough to assist the pastor in guarding the doctrine of the congregation from error.

From among the elders and deacons some will manifest the gift of teaching. Thorough Bible knowledge is a necessity for this ministry. Some of the most adept Bible teachers in the church today are laymen who have developed their gift by hard work and study.

A good beginning for the Bible study program would be the Book of Romans. This Pauline epistle is one of the most systematic presentations of the doctrine of Biblical salvation to be found in the whole Bible. It provides abundant resource for personal living and ministry basic to understanding the condition of man and God's provision through Christ for his redemption.

Learning to mark one's Bible and to write out notes on what has been learned from the passage help fix the truth in the student's mind. Your Bible study notes may not be professional but they are your own expression of truth. This practice helps one to think his way through until he can grasp the meaning of the passage.

Allotting time for memorizing key verses can equip the elder or deacon for more effective ministry. Learning a number of select verses relating to personal salvation, faith, prayer, and discipleship fits the leader for a ready counseling ministry. If memory work is too difficult, prepare a small notebook with these key verses written out or typed. One very successful personal soul winner in the midwest used this method. He was a businessman saved late in life, thus it was hard for him to memorize scripture, and he found that by writing out the verses he had them readily available. He later learned that those to whom he ministered were impressed that he had gone to the trouble of writing out the passages used in personal work. This method demonstrated the sincerity of this layman in the business of winning other men to Christ.

Principles of Leadership

Whatever else elders or deacons may be they are leaders among the people. To accomplish their role in the family of God they must learn the art of leading others. Everyone is not a leader. Those without leadership ability look to those who have it to give their ministry direction and oversight. This is the divine plan for the church.

Leadership by its very nature calls for people who can see ahead and plan for action. A leader must learn to dream dreams. He must be able to see by the eye of faith farther than the average member of the congregation. The work of God goes forward as a leader is willing to follow the vision given him by the Holy Spirit. He must be so sure of God's leading that he can walk by faith when the circumstances are difficult. A leader must have the quality of patience to wait for the people to fully understand the vision for expansion and outreach that races ahead of his own head. A leader must cultivate the art of leading people through periods of change. The actual implementations of any vision of enlarged ministry calls for change in the style and patterns of congregational life. Change almost always meets with resistance. The mark of a leader is to see the work through this stage and guide the people through the trauma of change. The pastor has no better support for these critical times than the skillful elders and deacons who are his helpers to see the project to ultimate completion. The core leadership must be responsible to steer the ship of Zion through the stormy waters of change.

To succeed in leadership one must have a working knowledge of why structures are needed for coordinating the work of the church. What are their functions? When should they be abandoned or changed? Since the church is in motion its structures are in constant need of adjustment. It is the leader's job to sense the need for these adjustments and to make them.

One is not necessarily a leader because he has been elected to a leadership position. He is not a leader just because he has gifts for leadership. Training, study, and experience are essential to making a leader. The gift for leadership is a precious commodity in the household of faith and it needs to be exercised and nurtured to the point of maximum usefulness. A self-study program becomes a part of this process. Good books on the art of Christian leadership should be read. A course or two should be taken in the church's *Christian Life and Ministry* series that relates to leadership.

Study People and Their Needs

Christian ministry always relates to people. Those members of the church body honored with the office of elder or deacon will find their primary function to be touching people for the sake of Christ and His church. Since the composition of any given congregation is varied by age, personality, and cultural background the church leader finds so many possibilities of relating to people. The variety of people in a church suggests that elders and deacons should specialize in a group or groups within the congregation.

An elder who has a keen interest in youth and has good rapport with them becomes an ideal unofficial liason between the youth of the congregation and its official leadership. This elder should read all about young people and their problems. Another elder may be drawn to senior citizens. He should study gereatrics to gain an understanding of the needs of the elderly and develop his ability to minister to them. A deacon finds himself attracted to the growing group of young married people in his church. They become a subject for his study and self-development. A deacon or elder might also feel a burden for certain areas of the church's ministry such as Christian education. His study and self-improvement program would include some sound books on the philosophy and the methodology of Christian education.

To assure continued personal growth and productivity of ministry in-service training is a must. Self-study is equally important. A wise lay leader will sign up for every available training course to strengthen his ministry and will supplement the church curriculum with a voluntary self-study program.

12

The Elders and Deacons and the Denomination

The local church cannot exist in a vacuum. It is a part of a larger fellowship, namely the district and the General Council. An elder cannot understand his local church until he understands it as a part of the greater whole. This perception will enlarge the vision and the interests of the lay elder. He will know how to be supportive of the pastor as he relates the work of the local church to the ministries and concerns of the denomination. The informed lay elder will also be able to make a contribution through his spiritual gifts that will be beneficial to the whole denomination.

The strength, integrity, and faithfulness of a denomination is determined by the level of participation on the part of its members. Lay-elders should be involved in the activities of the district and the general church body. The elders should be representatives of the very best lay leadership in the local churches. The denomination should be enriched by the contribution these elders make in ministry and action.

The lay-elder's ability to make good judgments regarding the local church program is to some degree dependent on his knowledge of the denomination and its program. He should know the services available to the local church from the denominational level.

A local church has a tendency to become selfish just as individual Christians may become self-centered. Its program and interests are focused on the welfare and maintenance of its own membership without consideration of the large Christian community of which it is a part. An ingrown church soon becomes torn with internal conflicts. The local church needs the services, the fellowship, the discipline, and the outreach which the larger denominational body provides.

Church Government

The government of the church of Jesus Christ is a spiritual issue. The basic guidelines for formulating church government are to be found in the scriptures. The principles of church government found in the Bible are so basic and broad as to serve the church in many different cultures and across many very different historical periods. Church history reveals three basic patterns of church government to have prevailed over the centuries. The Episcopal system confers authority upon the bishops and other properly ordained clergy to rule in both the local church situation and in the denomination as a whole. Where this system exists among Protestants it is a carry-over from Roman Catholicism.

Many of the Reformation churches developed Presbyterianism as their view of proper church government. Presbyterian comes from the Greek form of the word *elder*. This form of ecclesiastical government gives to the elders the oversight of the congregation and the higher level denominational structure. The eldership is divided into teaching elders and ruling elders.

Congregationalism is the third form of church government. It conceives of the local church as the only visibility the church enjoys. Each congregation is considered completely autonomous. It may belong to a fellowship or association of churches for the purpose of services and fellowship but is not obligated to the fellowship. The local church is completely free in matters of doctrine, clergy, and governance.

The Christian and Missionary Alliance has a government which incorporates some things from both congregationalism and presbyterianism. Basic to Alliance church government is the principle of constituted authority. The constitutional documents are all established by the General Council and are mandatory on the local churches. They may write their own by-laws providing they do not conflict with the constitution for churches found in the Manual of the Christian and Missionary Alliance. The local church relates to both the district and the general church body. The legislation of the General Council and the

106

District are mandatory for local churches. Each local church has the right of lay representation at District Conference and General Council. The official workers are also accredited delegates to these legislative bodies. The vitality and usefulness of these assemblies are determined by the leadership sent by local churches. Each congregation should send its best lay leaders to District Conference and General Council.

Local churches will find the exercise of their franchise in the denominational legislative assemblies a good investment of funds and time. It gives each church a legitimate platform for voicing its concerns and exerting its influence upon the total fellowship.

Attendence at these gatherings heightens the participant's viewpoint of the church and widens his horizons. The inspiration, instruction, and interaction of the larger church community provides an enriching experience.

The lay leadership in a local church need to be aware of the services provided by the denomination. All churches need certain services if they are to continue to operate. The local church needs oversight, resources for pastoral leadership, consultation in the event of internal problems, literature, camps and conferences, retreats for training and renewal, outlets for service at home and abroad. No church in the contemporary scene could afford to provide these services just for themselves. Independent congregations are forced to seek these services in the open market. Some of the most critical services are not readily available to these churches. A part of the rationale for the denominational structure is that it can provide such services more economically and at the same time allow the people receiving the services a voice in the government and policies of the particular service.

The obvious outcome of denominational structure is to impose some limitations on the autonomy of the local church. These limitations in no way impede a creative dynamic operation in the local church. They are designed to provide coordination in the mutual endeavors of the church. They also help assure quality and consistency in the leadership of the church.

In order to maintain harmony it is essential that the lay leaders and the pastor of each congregation have the same commitment to the Christian and Missionary Alliance. Elders and deacons

107

should have a basic understanding of the philosophy of government, the overall purposes, and the operational policies of the Christian and Missionary Alliance. They should keep aware of the work of the whole movement so as to lend support to that work as it relates to the local church.

The elders' or deacons' understanding of the church must be broad enough to take in the relationship of their own congregation to the other churches of the organization of which it is a part. There is also a place for extending that understanding to the whole evangelical community. As a local church cannot exist if cut off from its denomination neither can a denomination exist in isolation from all the rest of the people of God. Not only pastor but lay leaders must be knowledgable about what is happening across the world among Bible-believing Christians.

Some local church leadership has fallen into the error of substituting their concerns for trans-denominational activity in the place of denominational activity. This practice is nonproductive and tends to isolate that local church from its own fellowship. Persistence in this practice ultimately leads to altering of purpose and philosophy of ministry.

Denominational loyalty and unity can only be expected when the denomination maintains unswerving allegiance to the integrity of the Bible and sound doctrine.

Rules and Regulations

Out of the common experience of the Christian and Missionary Alliance has come a philosophy of ministry, a set of objectives, and the governing documents suited to the local church, the district and the headquarters level. Because some rules are of general concern they are published in the official *Manual* and made available to all who wish to study them. *The Manual of the Christian and Missionary Alliance* should be read carefully by every elder and deacon.

The elders will want to give their attention to the policies on discipline found in the manual. This document explains the scriptural basis for church discipline and outlines a procedure to assure the protection of the accused and also of the church and its officers. The principles discussed here provide the board of elders with essential guidelines for carrying out their responsibilities in matters of discipline.

The lay-elder should be thoroughly acquainted with the proper candidating procedure for calling a minister to his congregation. Internal difficulties often arise in a local church when the lay leadership has no knowledge of this procedure, and assuming there is no fixed method, they devise a system for securing candidates on their own. It is embarrassing and disruptive both to the local church leadership and to the district leadership when the two systems come into conflict.

Lay-elders often sit with the church executive committee as they interview pastoral candidates. Their insights and understanding of the spiritual needs of the congregation should be available to the executive committee as they choose a pastor. The elders' evaluation of the candidate should be sought by the church executive committee.

Stewardship

The stewardship pattern of a local church is affected by the denomination's programs for ministry. When lay leadership sits with pastoral leadership to plan an annual budget for the church the district and the denominational budgets should be given serious consideration.

The budget for the general fund of the Christian and Missionary Alliance is published annually and distributed to all the churches. A supplemental budget is also given for specialized ministries. The general fund budget is the resource out of which the administrative arm of the church operates as well as the overseas program. The specialized ministries budget pays both the administration and operation of ethnic ministry in North and Central America and the Carribean area. A minimum of sixty-four percent of the general fund must be allocated to overseas ministry. The high priority given to the general fund and specialized ministries income is underscored by the constitutional requirement that each local church maintain a separate treasury for general fund and specialized ministries giving and that the receipts be remitted to the headquarters office monthly.

Such a practice has more than tradition behind it. As a church body devoted to faith the Christian and Missionary Alliance has no large reserves of money from which to draw. The program is a month-by-month faith operation. God has greatly honored this faith approach to finances.

The lay leaders in the local church need to know that the missionary dollar is a necessity to achieving the level of world outreach to which this fellowship has pledged itself.

District Ministries

Districts have a legitimate claim on the giving of local churches because of the important contribution they make both to the local church and to the movement at large. Districts are responsible to provide direct services to the local churches within their geographical territory. The district superintendent provides the churches with viable ministerial candidates and gives valuable oversight to the local church during the critical days of the interim between pastors.

Districts provide the system for church planting. By experienced oversight and funding the district coordinates all the efforts of the existing churches to plant new churches. The better the lay-leadership is acquainted with the need for extension and how the district meets that need the stronger will be their support of district extension. Realizing that church planting is extension evangelism lay leaders will be ready to promote their own congregation mothering a new church.

Missionary Vision

Keeping the missionary vision alive is the responsibility of both elders and deacons. Their visibility as lay leaders gives them an opportunity to encourage wholehearted commitment on the part of the membership to reaching a lost world. The elders and deacons can provide a model of participation in missions by their prayer burden, their giving and their readiness to promote world missions. Elders and deacons should be knowledgable of the missionary program of the Christian and Missionary Alliance. How many fields are open? Where are they? What kinds of ministry do missionaries perform? What are the national churches like? What is the movement's missionary obligation?

Evangelism

The elders are especially involved in the church's evangelism program. The deacons and deaconesses also have an important role in reaching out to the lost. The tools made available by the denomination for visitation, personal soul-winning, sanctuary evangelism, and follow-up will prove helpful in training a work force for evangelism. The seminars or other training opportunities offered by the district or the offices of international headquarters help the core leaders of each local church to keep growing both in their spiritual experience and in their ministry.

The need for keeping good records of converts, baptisms, membership and church attendance takes on new meaning when leadership understands that a practical use is being made of these statistics. As the pastor informs his elders and deacons of district and national trends, patterns, and statistics of evangelism they feel a part of this overall process of evaluation.

Perspective

Keeping the local church lay leadership well informed as to what is happening in the denomination helps them keep their own work in perspective. It is easy for a local church to lose perspective because it compares itself with itself. The leaders need a larger frame of reference for evaluating their church and its activities.

Exposure to the programs of other churches in the district provides a valid base for comparison. Leadership may at times be deceived either as to the ineffectiveness or the effectiveness of what is taking place in their own church. The contacts with other churches is not only valuable for the purpose of better evaluation but some of the new ideas and methods introduced can be adopted to their local needs.

Leadership may be tempted to see the whole movement through the eyes of their local situation. The smallness, the weaknesses, the problems of their church seem to be the norm. They assume the same deadness and spiritual depression prevails everywhere. Such a church can be moved to fresh hope and vitality by discovering that God is at work in a congregation that had as many adverse problems as their own. Learning about the renewal and subsequent growth of a sister church may be the key to recovery for a depressed congregation. As mutual sharing blesses the local body of believers a similar mutuality of blessing exists among congregations of the larger church body. They strengthen and encourage one another.

The dictionary defines *perspective* as a view of things in their true relationship or relative importance. The pastor, elders, and deacons of any church must be able to judge the relative importance of each program and ministry of their local church and how its work relates to the whole church.

Paul S. Wright, a Presbyterian pastor, writing to instruct the ruling elders (lay-elders) of the churches of that denomination says,

> "No church will increase spiritual vitality within itself that is not growing in the range of its vision and outreach. To encourage the church in obedience to its Lord to undertake tasks beyond its own walk and to propose ways and means by which this shall be accomplished can be the most stimulating and exciting aspect of a ruling elder's work."[1]

Ministries

Lay-elders and deacons will discover the ministries provided by the district enriches the life of the local church. What church would not benefit from the summer camping and conference ministry? A recent survey disclosed that a high percentage of overseas missionaries heard and responded to the call of God at a summer youth camp. A comparable percentage of pastors were also called at summer camp.

The family Bible conference is a needed supplement to ministries a given church can offer to its families. What a blessing to spend several days free of routine responsibilities enjoying expository preaching and teaching, missionary education, and forceful evangelistic preaching. The concentration of the family Bible conference is an opportunity for people to deal with spiritual problems they tend to pass over at home. It is a healthy situation for parents and children to be together in a common experience. Youth and children's camps are valuable but cannot replace the unique ministry of the family conference.

The summer camp and conference ministry is strengthened by the presence and the participation of the elders and deacons from the local churches of the area or district. These church leaders in turn are better prepared for the work assigned them in the home church as a result of the camping experience. Family conferences may be the best opportunity for the elders or deacons to relate to all the members of the families that attend the conference. In a relaxed atmosphere they can fellowship with the children, youth, and adults of each family.

Alliance Men's Retreats provide another contact for local church lay leaders. The men should be encouraged to be active in the local Alliance Men's group and the retreats offered by the district. Elders and deacons do well to support this important ministry. It is the best means of encouraging the laymen to move from the position of spectators in the church's program to active participants. The men's organization is a dynamic force for evangelism. It awakens men to see how they can personally relate to the worldwide missionary outreach. Elders and deacons will best encourage other laymen by being a vital part of this movement in the church.

The district conference or superintendent at times will ask elders or deacons to serve on committees related to the district ministries. This experience opens up new insights and sharpens the skills of local church lay leaders. The district needs the help of the best lay leadership. The most urgent need in the contemporary evangelical church is to bring to life and to set in action the mighty force of the church's laity. Since elders and deacons are such important core leaders they set the example for other laymen to get involved in the Lord's work.

Lay preachers are more important than ever in the history of the church. Rapid church growth requires many workers. The formal system of pastoral training at its top production cannot keep up with rapid church growth. The secret of growth is to have a work force large enough to keep up with the rate of church planting. This can only be accomplished by the utilization of lay preachers. The awakened church will have a concern to mother new congregations. This can be accomplished in many instances by assigning a gifted lay-elder or a deacon to the preaching responsibility and pastoral duties of the new group. Modern church growth experts have discovered lay preaching to be alive wherever the church is having rapid advance.

Elders and deacons will find the discovery of what the Christian and Missionary Alliance is doing in the world to be challenging. They will find in the ministries of their district another door of opportunity. Their personal lives and that of the church they serve will be richer as a result of this relationship to the whole church.

---

[1] Paul S. Wright, *The Duties of the Ruling Elder,* The Westminster Press, Philadelphia, 1952, p. 80.

13

The Election and Consecration of Elders and Deacons

The first church election took place in the upper room as the one hundred and twenty waited for the outpouring of the Holy Spirit. In the course of their praying, heart searching and study of the scripture God moved upon Peter to address the group.

And at this time Peter stood up in the midst of the brethren (a gathering of about one hundred and twenty persons was there together), and said,

"Brethren, the Scripture had to be fulfilled, with the Holy Spirit foretold by the mouth of David concerning Judas, who became a guide to those who arrested Jesus.

For he was counted among us, and received his portion in this ministry."

(Now this man acquired a field with the price of his wickedness; and falling headlong, he burst open in the middle and all his bowels gushed out.

And it became known to all who were living in Jerusalem; so that in their own language that field was called Hakeldama, that is, Field of Blood).

"For it is written in the book of Psalms,
'Let his homestead be made desolate,
And let no man dwell in it'; and,
'His office let another man take.'

"It is therefore necessary that of the men who have accompanied us all the time that the Lord Jesus went in and out among us—

beginning with the baptism of John, until the day that He was taken up from us—one of these should become a witness with us of His resurrection."

115

And they put forward two men, Joseph called Barsabbas (who was also called Justus), and Matthias.

And they prayed, and said, "Thou, Lord, who knowest the hearts of all men, show which one of these two Thou hast chosen

to occupy this ministry and apostleship from which Judas turned aside to go to his own place."

And they drew lots for them, and the lot fell to Matthias; and he was numbered with the eleven apostles. (Acts 1:15-26)

In this simple account lies a solid foundation for the whole theology of church elections. It may come as a surprise to some believers that the church's annual meeting is scriptural and deserves much more attention than it usually gets. In far too many churches the election of officers is of little concern to the majority of the congregation. The quality and the credibility of lay leadership depends on the church selecting such officers in a manner and an attitude worthy of the scriptures.

Peter addressed the group as brothers. The apostle was emphasizing the unity of the community of disciples—they were a brotherhood; they were one in concern and spirit. An atmosphere of oneness is essential for the sacred responsibility of electing the church's officers and leaders. The membership should be reminded weeks in advance of the election to provide time for personal prayer and heart searching as to each individual's attitude toward the brotherhood. It is impossible to arrive at the mind of God when warring factions are seeking their own interests. The first spiritual preparation of the assembly before an election is to promote unity.

Peter's second concern as he stood before the disciples was that the election be carried out according to the Word of God. The scriptures are the source of doctrine as well as the source of practice. The guidelines for effective church leadership are to be found in the scriptures. Peter advised the assembly that an election to fill the vacancy left by the backsliding of Judas was a divine directive.

May another take his place of leadership. (Psa. 109:8)

The leadership of the church should not be just the product of social evolution or the perpetuation of a traditional system. The offices of church leadership must be justified by the scriptures. Most congregations need instruction as to what the Bible has to say about the offices and the leaders of the church.

The qualifications for the office were carefully explained by Peter. Not just any member of the congregation could be nominated to fill the office. Only qualified candidates could be considered. The modern practice of selecting leaders is not always done so carefully. Some people are considered with the hope they will get involved in the church. Others are named with view to passing the responsibilities around to more people. In some elections people are proposed for office because they have good personalities. It is not at all uncommon in some churches for offices to be given out as a sort of reward for faithfulness. Such a mentality with regard to church elections betrays a total disregard for Biblical qualifications. The lay leadership problems are no longer a mystery when the system by which they have been selected is understood.

In nominating committee and the whole membership should be instructed as to the proper qualifications for each office. This information should be given well in advance of the election. Every person considered for the office should be measured by the qualification necessary to carry out the work of the office.

The Jerusalem congregation made its nominations after thoughtful consideration of the qualifications for the apostolic office. The church election is a time for both the guidelines of parlimentary procedure and scriptural principle to be applied. The constitution allows for nominations to be made from the floor. That such a privilege is extended the whole body is appropriate, but it does require responsibility. Nominations should not be made from the top of the head and on the spur of the moment. Any member who places a name in nomination should give much thought and prayer to the matter. They should be sure this individual they wish to nominate meets the qualifications required for the office. They should also contact the individual as to their willingness to assume the office if elected. These procedures should be followed for all elected positions but they are especially important as they apply to elders and deacons.

After the assembly in Jerusalem proposed their nominees

they went to prayer. The precedent set by the first church should be observed by modern congregations. At every crisis of leadership in the New Testament the church went to prayer. What better way to recognize Christ's leadership over His church. A praying congregation is obviously a dependent one. In faith and humility they seek the mind of Christ. Special prayer meetings preceding the church election are still in order. In the homes of the membership the selection of the church's officers should be a subject of family prayer.

There is a suggestion as to the petition in particular that the church should pray when she seeks direction in the choosing of her officers.

> . . . *Thou, Lord, knowest the hearts of all men, show which one of these two Thou hast chosen. (Acts 1:24)*

That which most fits a man for the service of Christ is the true state of his heart. Christ alone knows the heart of a man. No pretense is possible with Him. Christ can best make the choice for He knows the heart. Though Christ brings His people into the process of selecting leadership He does so in the context of faith and prayer. Christ is seen as ultimately making the choice for the church. Church elections would soon be changed from a boring duty to a delightful spiritual exercise if the fellowship took to heart these simple biblical guidelines.

The practice of the early Christians indicates divine approval for the process of engaging the congregation in the selection of their officers. There were a few exceptions to this practice and all of these were associated with newly-established churches. Paul or one of his missionary coworkers would in these pioneer churches appoint the first eldership for the assembly. With the maturation of the church the whole congregation became involved in selecting the officers. This was true of both the elders and deacons.

The Laying On of Hands

Just as the New Testament scriptures lay down guiding principles for the selection of office-bearers scripture also speaks to the church's right to commission their officers. The formal setting apart of leaders before the whole assembly has a very ancient precedent. From the beginning of Israel as a covenant nation God has blessed the rite of the laying on of hands as a symbol of the act of commissioning God's servants.

When Moses was to lay down his administrative responsibility God selected Joshua to take Moses' position as leader. The Lord instructed Moses to ordain Joshua by the laying on of hands.

> So the Lord said to Moses, "Take Joshua the son of Nun, a man in whom is the Spirit, and lay your hand on him"; . . . Then he laid his hands on him and commissioned him, just as the Lord had spoken through Moses. (Num. 27:18, 23)

For the full-time pastor-elder the church's commission is called ordination. While it differs from the laying on of hands to consecrate elders and deacons, ordination differs only in degree. Those ministers ordained by the district ordaining council have a different commitment than lay leaders. They have different gifts related to their function as the pastor of the flock or in a larger ministry among the churches.

There is a sense in which the consecration of the elders and the deacons is a step above the consecration of all other lay leaders in the local church. Scripture especially authorizes the laying on of hands with these two offices by its record of early church practice. The elders and deacons make a commitment that is higher than most lay workers make to the ministry of Christ's church. They must, therefore, not only be carefully selected but they should be publicly commissioned for their work.

A careful study of the scriptural use of the laying on of hands is rewarding. This rite has come to symbolize the spiritual process of setting one apart for sacred ministry. When the pastor and lay-elders and deacons lay their hands on the newly-elected elders and deacons the act symbolizes the communication with the whole assembly. It symbolizes not just the officials but the whole body's recognition of their qualifications and calling to serve Christ in their important church offices.

The laying on of hands is frequently associated with the communication of the Holy Spirit.

> *But select from among you, brethren, seven men of good reputation, full of the Spirit and of wisdom, whom we may put in charge of this task.*
> *And the statement found approval with the whole congregation; and they chose Stephen, a man full of faith and of the Holy Spirit, and Philip, Prochorus, Nicanor, Timon, Parmenas and Nicolas, a proselyte from Antioch.*
> *And these they brought before the apostles; and after praying, they laid their hands on them. (Acts 6:3, 5-6)*

The practice of confirmation in the Anglican, Lutheran and Reformation churches is a continuation of this ancient church rite. They laid hands on new believers and prayed that they might be filled with the Holy Spirit. It can therefore be concluded that the laying on of hands in commissioning church officers symbolizes the expectation that they be filled with the Holy Spirit and given any gifts needed to fulfill their ministry.

Jesus used the laying on of hands to symbolize the conferring of a blessing.

> *And He took them in His arms and began blessing them, laying His hands upon them. (Mark 10:16)*

Certainly the elected officers of the church need rich measures of spiritual grace and blessing to live godly lives and to lead the church of God. It should be expected that at the laying on of hands the recipients would experience a deepening of their spiritual lives.

There can also be a subjective effect from the commissioning service. It can serve to confirm the heart of the newly-elected elder that he has accepted this ministry in the will of God. The public laying on of hands may promote faith and expectation in the heart of the elder or deacon. He senses in a new way the oneness and the strength which comes from their mutual support. It reinforces the awesome responsibility of these offices. Elders and deacons are commissioned by the congregation and therefore accountable to it.

Care must be taken to avoid giving a mere sacredotal meaning to the ceremony of the laying on of hands. It is a symbolic action meant to speak not only to those upon whom it is performed but to the audience as well. It is more than an official commissioning; it is an act of consecration. Both God and His servant have a role to carry out in true consecration. The kneeling servant must from the depths of his heart dedicate all he is and ever hopes to be to the service of Christ. God in turn responds to that dedication by filling the waiting servant with a deep assurance that his dedication is acceptable to God. God sets the Spirit's seal on true dedication enabling the servant of the Lord to minister faithfully and fruitfully for Christ.

The Church's Attitude Toward Its Officers

There is an association between the public laying on of hands and the church family's acceptance of the ministry of the elders and the deacons. The offices of the church are by this means elevated above office bearing in other institutions. The officers of Christ's church are anointed to rule and lead. In the government of God's house anointing and authority can never be divorced without the church losing the blessing of spiritual authority. The membership responds to their officers not because they hold the position of authority but because they are anointed to serve.

The church of Jesus Christ on earth recognizes her risen Lord as seated in majesty on high. The exalted Head of the church and the Wellspring of all authority oversees His church on earth as a Chief Shepherd. Since He is bodily absent from His house Christ has placed His most trusted servants in charge. Whatever else the laying on of hands may symbolize it speaks of the authority of the head of the church conferred on humble servants until their Lord returns.

D. D. Bannerman, Scotch theologian of the last century, says of the commissioning of elders,

"The presbyters are formally set apart to their office in the church, with solemn religious services."[1]

The pastor, the lay-elders and the deacons should participate in the commissioning of new elders and deacons. This service may well be a part of a regular Sunday Morning Worship. It is an ideal occasion for a sermon on the qualifications of the elders and the deacons along with a description of their ministry. The recently-elected officers should be invited to the front of the church and introduced to the congregation. The pastor or a lay-elder selected for the occasion will direct a series of questions to these officers. The answers given will be a public witness of the officers' qualifications, spiritual dedication, and complete loyalty to the church. The following questions would serve the purpose of this part of the ceremony:

1. Do you know Jesus Christ as your personal Lord and Saviour and have you determined to serve Him with all of your heart?

2. Do you accept the inspiration and the authority of the scriptures and are you willing they should be the only rule for faith and practice?

3. Have you read the Statement of Faith of the Christian and Missionary Alliance and do you accept it without reservation as being consistent with the Word of God and a summary of those things most surely believed among us?

4. Have you read the various constitutions of the Christian and Missionary Alliance and are you willing to be governed by constituted authority as represented by the regulations and policies of the Christian and Missionary Alliance?

5. Are you willing to study and train for the ministry to which the church has elected you? Will you seek by diligent service and godly living to promote the spiritual welfare of this church?

6. Do you have a burden for lost souls and are you willing to engage in personal soul-winning?

7. Have you acquainted yourself with the worldwide missionary outreach of the church and will you pledge your strength toward the realizing of this objective?

Having posed these questions and received clear answers, the elders and the deacons being commissioned should kneel at the altar for the laying on of hands. The pastor or a lay-elder he selects will pray the dedicatory prayer. Such a public dedication of church officers heightens the importance with which each individual member views office bearing. It also moves the congregation to think on the seriousness of serving Christ and also the privilege it is to serve Him.

The Accountability of Officers

The formal public laying on of hands will linger in the minds of the elected officers for years to come reminding them that their accountability to the congregation that elected them is only the introduction of a greater accountability. It is one thing to be accountable to men; it is another thing to be accountable to Christ. Each elder and deacon will some day stand before Christ to give an account. Those servants Christ places in charge of His house He holds accountable to Him for their ministry.

---

[1] D. D. Bannerman, *The Scripture Doctrine of the Church*, Baker Book House, Grand Rapids, Reprint of 1887 edition issued in Edinburgh, p. 538.

Servants in Charge

Leader's Guide

Introduction

The contemporary Church is experiencing a fresh concern for the integrity of the offices of elder and deacon. Many church members and even church officers have had no clear understanding of the role of these important servants of the church. These positions have become encrusted with church tradition, and the time has come to recover their true meaning from the New Testament.

Servants in Charge, in addition to providing a manual for training church officers, also addresses the theological roots of those offices. It is necessary for each elder and deacon to understand the implications of accepting God's call and the church's call to these ministries. This course of study may in some instances invoke serious heart searching, and the teacher must be prepared to guide the group through such experiences. If church officers have not been serious in seeking to understand their responsibilities, these lessons should help them assume such a concern.

The senior pastor is the ideal teacher for this course. If the church is large enough to have a multiple pastoral staff, another qualified member of the pastoral staff could be selected as the teacher. An experienced lay elder could also teach this course.

The course may be taught as often as new personnel is added to the presbytery and diaconate of the local church. If such training has not been previously provided by the church, all elders, deacons and deaconesses should be given the training.

Churches may find it wise to hold their annual election at least a quarter before the new officers assume their duties, allowing time for the training course.

The course may also be opened to members that show an interest in the eldership or the ministry of deacons. They will receive an advanced understanding of what the Scriptures and the church require of the believers privileged to serve these offices.

It is advisable that the wives of the elders and deacons take the training course along with their husbands. Single deaconesses should also attend the course. The ministry of the women requires the same high standard of character, the impartation of spiritual gifts and the careful preparation expected of all lay ministries in the church.

At an appropriate time during the thirteen weeks required for this course, a suggested agenda for a board of elders, a board of deacons and the deaconesses could be distributed to the class. A simulated meeting might help the class understand the importance, the order and the subject matter of a good meeting.

Discuss with the class the reporting system used in your local church. How do the elders report? How does the deacon board report? It is a good practice to require a monthly report to the pastor and the church executive board. It should be in writing.

Every effort should be made to relate the lessons to the realities of life and ministry in the church. The class leaders are responsible to adapt the studies to the particular needs in their local congregation.

1

Local Church Leadership

Purpose of the Lesson

The place of leadership in the Church has been established by the Scriptures. There are some aspects of Christian leadership that are comparable with leadership in any other organization. But the leaders of the household of faith also have qualities quite unique to their task. The attitude of those placed in charge of Christ's work reflects a different spirit than the authority figures of the secular world. Christ's leaders are servants whose chief credential for ministry is spiritual in nature. The pastor, elders and deacons constitute a basic leadership core. These officers of the church look for and cultivate those members with gifts for leadership in the assembly.

Questions for Discussion

1. How were the leaders of Israel chosen for their tasks?
2. Is a divine call to leadership necessary?
3. Why does the church need leaders?
4. How do the Scriptures suggest a ratio of leaders to workers?
5. What are some of the benefits of multiple leadership in the congregation?

6. Explore from as many sources as possible the meaning of the word *ministry*.
7. Compare the Gentile concept of a servant with that of the Jews.
8. How would you demonstrate from Scripture that Jesus left a plan of leadership with His Church?
9. Describe the attitude Jesus taught should characterize leaders.
10. What happens when leadership becomes isolated from service?
11. What does the Bible mean by the directive "Obey your leaders"? (Hebrews 13:17)
12. How do spiritual gifts relate to leadership?

The Teaching Plan

Divide the class into four groups with appointed leaders. Ask each group to reflect on Exodus 18:17-26 and from that passage compile a list of principles governing church leadership. A time block of at least fifteen minutes should be allowed. Return the class to a full session and ask each leader in turn to share the results of his or her group's discussion. Use the blackboard or overhead projector to make a composite of these principles.

Lead the class through a discussion of basic core leadership. Make sure they understand this concept. Give special attention to the relationship of core leadership with all other church leadership.

Resource Material

Engstrom, Ted. W. *The Making of a Christian Leader*. Grand Rapids: Zondervan, 1977.

Gangel, Kenneth O. *Competent to Lead*. Chicago: Moody Press, 1974.

Sanders, J. Oswald. *Spiritual Leadership.* Chicago: Moody Press, 1976.

2

Who Is the Pastor?

Purpose of the Lesson

The Scripture says that Christ has given some to the Church to be pastors. The pastoral function in the New Testament includes the general oversight of the congregation and the shepherd care of its membership. For the sake of good order and efficiency a pastor-elder should serve as the constituted head of each congregation. The pastoral office is usually a full-time responsibility requiring certain spiritual gifts, training and certification by the general church body. This chapter combines the scriptural background with the practical functions of the pastoral office and points out the similarities and the differences between the pastoral role and that of other church officers.

Questions for Discussion

1. What does the term *pastor* suggest about leadership in the church?
2. Are all gifted leaders assigned to local churches or do some gifted leaders serve the Church at large?
3. What gifts are needed for the pastoral ministry?
4. What is the usual training given to pastors in The Christian and Missionary Alliance?

5. Explain the in-service training given by the district in preparation for ordination. Discuss the value of this process.
6. Make a list of the responsibilities of the pastor in the local church.
7. What are his denominational responsibilities? How do they enrich his ministry?
8. How does a pastor-elder differ from a lay-elder?
9. What is the church's responsibility toward its pastor?
10. What biblical and historical evidence is there that the Protestant tradition of the pastoral office is correct?

The Teaching Plan

The pastoral concept first appears in the Old Testament. The twenty-third psalm described God's care over His people in pastoral terms. The leadership role of Moses reflects that of the shepherd. The analogy was meaningful to Israel, for they were shepherds. God is the Chief Shepherd and His appointed leaders are the undershepherds.

The New Testament writers bring the pastoral concept into focus. Ephesians 4:11-12 provides the key passage for understanding the role of the pastor in the church. The emphasis of this passage is upon the pastor as a person rather than a function. Christ gives the pastor to the church.

It is important for the members of the class to work through the biblical basis of the pastoral office.

The cultural role of the pastor adds the dimension of his education, in-service training, credentials and ordination. Many lay leaders have not been exposed to the process by which the church prepares and certifies its pastors. An understanding of this procedure will help fill out their concept of the pastoral office.

Emphasis should also be given to the distinct functions of the pastor and how they differ from the functions of lay leaders. Attention should be given to those functions which may be shared by both pastor-elder and lay-elders.

Each ordained minister on a multiple church staff is a pastor-elder, since his function in the church is on a par with that of the senior pastor. The unique position of the senior pastor in this structure should be discussed.

A thorough exposition of First Timothy 5:17-19 would make a good foundation for this lesson. All of the above points of emphasis emerge in the passage.

Resource Material

Bannerman, D. Douglas. *The Scripture Doctrine of the Church.* Reprint of 1887 Edinburgh edition. Grand Rapids: Baker Book House.

MacNair, Donald J. *The Growing Local Church.* Grand Rapids: Baker Book House, 1975.

Perry, Lloyd. *Getting the Church on Target.* Chicago: Moody Press, 1977.

Stott, John R.W. *The Preacher's Portrait.* Grand Rapids: William B. Eerdman, 1972.

3

Who Are the Elders?

Purpose of the Lesson

This chapter seeks to define the office of eldership by examining the use of the term across the centuries of biblical history. The differences and similarities between Old Testament elders and New Testament elders show a progressive unfolding of the concept. The definition of an elder is further sharpened by exploring in the original languages the meaning of the term and its synonyms. A look at the words *elder* and *bishop* as understood in both the Jewish and Gentile culture of the New Testament period adds some helpful insights into the meaning of the office.

Questions for Discussion

1. What principle is Paul getting at when he lists addiction to wine as disqualifying a man for eldership?
2. What is to be the elder's attitude toward money according to the Scriptures?
3. What kind of home life did Paul expect elders to have?
4. Explain the importance of elders having a good reputation in the community.
5. Describe the disposition of an ideal elder.

6. Why should new converts not be considered for the office of elder?
7. What should a man do who feels an inner desire to be an elder?
8. What leadership qualities should an elder possess?
9. How would you describe the spiritual qualities needed for the eldership?
10. Why is it important for elders to be knowledgeable in the Scriptures and in doctrine?

The Teaching Plan

This lesson provides an opportunity to discuss the unique role of the lay-elders in the local church. The concept of a plurality of elders is evident in the New Testament. Church bodies have not all agreed as to the interpretation of this fact. Read Appendix A and share with the class the three most common interpretations of eldership among Protestants, showing the rationale for the view held by The Christian and Missionary Alliance. Make sure the relationship between pastor-elders and lay-elders is understood.

Emphasis should be placed on the importance of lay-elders in the contemporary church. Guide the class through a discussion of the relevance of elders to modern church life.

The eldership continues because it is a God-given plan for local church leadership. Discuss with the class the adverse effects of neglecting this plan. Suggest the following and encourage the class to add to the list.

1. Poor discipleship

2. Inadequate pastoral care of members

3. Overworked pastors

4. Lack of an overall development of leaders

Resource Material

Osterhaven M. Eugene. *The Spirit of the Reformed Tradition.* Grand Rapids: William B. Eerdman, 1971.

Wright, Paul S. *The Duties of the Ruling Elder.* Philadelphia: Westminster Press, 1972.

4

Who Are the Deacons?

Purpose of the Lesson

Since many modern church members have little or no conception of the dignity and the importance of the office of deacon, this chapter aims at giving an expanded definition of the deaconship drawing from both the Scriptures and church history. The lesson emphasizes the validity of the work of deacons and urges the development of their office to take in all the Scripture implies regarding it.

Questions for Discussion

1. What does the word *deacon* mean?
2. Under what circumstances were the first deacons appointed?
3. Why are spiritual qualifications important for the office of deacon?
4. Why is the ministry of deacons often associated with poverty?
5. What do the New Testament epistles teach regarding deacons?
6. What evidence is there that the deacons and elders worked together in the early church?
7. Was the ministry of the deacon in apostolic times limited to the care of material things?

8. How would modern deacons compare with Stephen and Philip?
9. What were the strengths of Stephen that made him a good deacon?
10. Other than waiting on tables, what ministries did deacons have in the early church?

The Teaching Plan

Evangelical churches often either have no deacons or take a low view of the position when it does exist. Lay leaders need help in understanding the importance of the deacon in the life of the church. It is one of two offices specified by Scripture for the local assembly. This study provides an opportunity to build on the foundation laid in the first two chapters. Organization directed by the Holy Spirit and conformed to the guidelines of Scripture is a blessing. Officers are essential for organization to function. A church officer is a leader selected by the congregation to give direction to the work.

The office of deacon came about when the workload required a division of responsibilities. Some leaders would specialize in the ministry of compassion. Their work at times would overlap. They were so closely related in ministry that the work was as one unit.

The class would profit from the exercise of drafting as a group an expanded definition of a deacon.

Resource Material

Nichols, Harold. *The Work of the Deacons and Deaconesses.* Valley Forge: Judson Press, 1975.

5

The Leadership Team

Purpose of the Lesson

In chapter 2 the core leadership concept was introduced. The core group is composed of the pastor-elder, the lay-elders and the deacons. These leaders must be unified as a team to have effective ministry. The core leadership must also be able to fit into the larger team called the church executive board. It has been the experience of many churches in arriving at a valid eldership to have tensions develop within the total organization of the congregation. This chapter attempts to find basic principles to govern this situation. A rationale is given for the existence of the church board and discusses the interaction between church officers.

The issues covered in this lesson are among the most important in this course of study.

Questions for Discussion

1. How does a church determine if its organizational structures are scriptural?
2. Does the New Testament give principles of church government or patterns of church government, or both?
3. What is a church executive board?

4. Should all the deacons and elders be on the board?
5. Is the dividing line between the responsibilities of the elder and deacon clear-cut or do they interchange at some points?
6. What bearing does the legal status of a church have upon its organizational structure?
7. What are the advantages and disadvantages of separate boards of elders and deacons?
8. How can an executive board reduce tensions in the operations of a local church?
9. Does the existence of a church board composed of several kinds of officers compromise any spiritual principles?
10. Does the church executive board have any precedent in church history?

The Teaching Plan

The class should read in advance of this lesson the constitution for a local church in the Manual of The Christian and Missionary Alliance. Since as a church body the Alliance has adopted this pattern of government, the lay leadership needs to understand how it relates to biblical principles.

A block of time should be provided for group discussion of the local church constitution and its relationship to the content of the lesson. (A non-Alliance church using the course could substitute its own local constitution.)

The relationship of the board of elders to the executive board needs explanation. Some feel that the subjugation of the decisions of the board of elders to the church executive board comprises the work of elders. A number of modern church renewal writers advocate a sovereign eldership for the local church. That position does not allow for congregational government if it is consistently carried out. The elders under that system would have total autonomy. But the practice of election by the congregation implies accountability to the congregation. If the elders are amenable to the congregation, then it is consistent for them to be amenable to the highest executive body of the congregation, the church executive board.

Resource Material

Current Manual of The Christian and Missionary Alliance.

Kirby, M.A. *Leadership.* (Understanding Bible Teaching Series.) London: Scripture Union, 1978.

Lightfoot, J.B. *The Apostolic Fathers.* Reprint of 1891 edition by MacMillan and Company, London. Grand Rapids: Baker Book House.*

MacNair, Donald J. *The Birth, Care and Feeding of a Local Church.* Grand Rapids: Baker Book House, 1976.**

* This book provides examples of early church practice as it relates to a combined board.

** MacNair approaches the board from his denomination's perspective providing helpful insight into the concept.

6

The Scriptural Qualifications of Elders

Purpose of the Lesson

This lesson is an analysis of the two lists of qualifications for the office of elders found in the pastoral epistles. The qualities have been grouped into five major categories, the composite of which is the image of an ideal elder.

Questions for Discussion

1. What significance did the apostle Paul place on the qualifications of an elder?
2. To what responsibility had Timothy and Titus been assigned which would make this information important?
3. Are there both human factors and divine factors operative in the calling of elders?
4. Are these qualifications relevant to modern church leaders?
5. What personal qualities should an elder possess?
6. Is being godly the only prerequisite for eldership?
7. Why is the elder's family situation so important?
8. Why do you think recent converts are barred from this office?

9. Discuss the importance of the elder's temperament.
10. Why should elders show leadership capabilities?

The Teaching Plan

This lesson is based on First Timothy 3:1-7 and Titus 1:5-9. Some attention should be given to the fact that these separate lists exist. Why is one passage addressed to the bishop and the other to elders? Reference should be made to chapter 3 where the two kinds of elders are pointed out. It is probable that the first list is to be addressed to elders with a pastoral role and the second to the lay-elders. The emphasis of this study should be upon the similarities of the two lists.

No double standard existed in the New Testament church. The same high qualifications were to be applied regardless of the kinds of leaders or their position in the structure.

Resource Material

Eerdman, Charles R. *The Pastoral Epistles.* Philadelphia: Westminster Press, 1976.

Getz, Gene A. *The Measure of a Man.* Glendale: Gospel Light, 1975.

Lindsay, Thomas M. *The Church and the Ministry in the Early Centuries.* Minneapolis: Klock and Klock (reprint).

7

The Scriptural Qualifications
of Deacons

Purpose of the Lesson

The deacons set apart by the early church had to meet
certain prescribed spiritual qualifications. The importance
of this office was accentuated by the standards set for
those elected to serve. This lesson examines the two
passages in the New Testament relating to the qualifications of the diaconate. The similarities as well as the differences between these qualities for leadership and
those addressed to the elders are carefully noted. Paul
included the women in his instructions for those church
leaders assigned to the ministries of compassion. The
spiritual character of such women must be equal to that
required of deacons.

Questions for Discussion

1. What situation in the Jerusalem church prompted the
   leadership to elect deacons?
2. What evidence is there that the selection of deacons
   met with divine approval?
3. What does it mean to have a good reputation in today's culture?

4. Why would the deacons' reputation in the community be important?
5. Why should the deacons be Spirit-filled men?
6. How would you interpret the word *dignity* in the modern context?
7. Why would it be wise for the deacons to have a high sense of stewardship?
8. What are some of the possible dangers of placing men into deaconship who are not spiritually ready for the task?
9. What impresses you as different about the qualifications of a deacon and those of an elder?
10. From the Scriptures, how would you construct the profile of a deaconess?

The Teaching Plan

The teacher will find it helpful to compose a harmony of the scriptural qualifications of elders and deacons. These could be placed in parallel columns for the purpose of comparison. Underscore each quality found under both offices. These qualities deserve an in-depth study. The use of a blackboard or an overhead projector will help the class visualize these important comparisons. Emphasis should be placed on the fact that the same high qualities prevail for every office of the church. Some churches tend to look upon deacons as relatively unimportant. Lead the class in a discussion of this issue. Help them to see the relationship between the high standards set by Scripture and the importance of the office.

This lesson provides a splendid opportunity to discuss the role of women in the church. While the deaconess was not a church office in the New Testament era it was an important ministry. The class would be enriched by including the wives of deacons and elders and any other women involved in church leadership. The qualifications for women who minister are the same as for men. Are women more often willing to minister than men? What qualities do women have that especially fit them for the church's ministries of compassion?

Resource Material

Christians, Clifford, Schippes, Earl, Smeoes. *Who in the World?* Grand Rapids: William B. Eerdman, 1972.

Howell, R.B.C. *The Deaconship, Its Nature, Qualifications, Relations and Rules.* Valley Forge: Judson Press, 1946.

Nichols, Harold. *The Work of the Deacon and Deaconess.* Valley Forge: Judson Press, 1975.

8

The Ministry of Lay-Elder

Purpose of the Lesson

Many lay-elders have not been given instruction as to the specific job they are to carry out. The Scripture gives the definition of an elder and some general principles governing his function, but the church must apply those principles in any given time or place. This lesson explores some possibilities for lay-elders' ministry in the contemporary church. Each church will not follow this identical pattern. Other alternatives could be added to fit the particular needs of a congregation.

Questions for Discussion

1. Why should the work of a lay-elder be part of a team operation?
2. What are the pitfalls of individualism for lay-elders?
3. Under what category can most of the work of a lay-elder be found?
4. Give a rationale for having a membership committee composed of lay-elders.
5. Should some of the elders specialize in the ministry of healing or should all of them be involved in it?
6. How should the disciplinary procedure be carried out?

7. What are some of the benefits of lay-elders visiting the membership of the church?
8. How can such a ministry be supportive of the pastor-elder?
9. What can lay-elders do to promote evangelism in the congregation?
10. What could be done to make the ministry of the lay-elders at the Lord's Table more meaningful?
11. What potential is there for preaching by lay-elders in your congregation and community?

The Teaching Plan

This lesson would be ideal for considering the job description of a lay-elder. Use the one your church leadership has developed. If the church does not have a job description for this office, use the sample found in Appendix B. Give the class a few minutes to read it before the discussion. Examine the job description as a class to determine if it fits the scriptural concept and the church constitution. Is it a strong or weak job description? Does it offer the services needed by your congregation? What ministries should be added? Are some functions outdated and ineffective? Is the lay-elder board large enough to carry out the workload?

Resource Material

Asquith, Glen H. *Church Officers at Work*. Valley Forge: Judson Press, 1977.

Getz, Gene A. *Sharpening the Focus of the Church*. Chicago: Moody Press, 1976.

MacNair, Donald J. *The Growing Local Church*. Grand Rapids: Baker Book House.

9

The Ministry of Deacons

Purpose of the Lesson

The New Testament pattern for developing church leadership was to institute ministries when they were needed. Church offices were functions rather than positions. How many men have been elected to the position of deacon without being introduced to the function for which the office is meant? The modern church needs deacons because the needs for that kind of ministry are present. This lesson attempts to suggest some areas where twentieth-century deacons are relevant.

Questions for Discussion

1. How would you distinguish the work of a deacon from that of a lay-elder?
2. What does the word *minister* teach the church about the nature of the diaconate?
3. Do the responsibilities of lay-elders and deacons ever overlap? How may they be correlated?
4. What functions did deacons have in New Testament times?
5. Are the ancient functions of a deacon applicable to our day?

6. What community needs do you see that would require the attention of the deacons?
7. What would the deacons' work be in an affluent church that had no poor people?
8. How could the ministry of the deacons improve the stewardship of the local church?
9. Do deacons have a spiritual ministry? Illustrate.
10. In what areas of church life do the deacons have a leadership role?

The Teaching Plan

Open the lesson with a brief survey of the biblical passages relating to the work of deacons. Attempt to draw from this background some broad guidelines for the deacons' ministry. Use these guidelines as a checklist for reviewing the deacons' job description. If your church does not have a written job description use the example in Appendix C.

Since the deacons often have an outreach ministry, guide the class in a consideration of the needs of your town, country, city or neighborhood. A map on a flip chart, overhead or roughed out on the blackboard could be used to make the study graphic. Indicate on the map ethnic, socio-economic and other groupings in the community. Pinpoint the geriatric institutions, homes for children, jails and prisons, transients' work camps and other situations where ministry might bring relief and blessing to needy people. How effectively is your church touching these needs now? What have been the lasting spiritual results from these ministries?

The class should also survey the needs within the congregation. Are the shut-ins being cared for? Do the deacons and deaconesses have regular ministry to the elderly? Are there handicapped people that are neglected?

In order to keep the task of this office in perspective, the place of deacons in the spiritual ministry of the church should be reviewed. A healthy diaconate should maintain a balance between their ministries of compassion and their spiritual service.

Resource Material

Haney, David. *The Idea of the Laity*. Grand Rapids: Zondervan Publishing House, 1975.

MacNair, Donald J. *The Growing Local Church*. Grand Rapids: Baker Book House.

Nichols, Harold. *The Work of the Deacon and Deaconess*. Valley Forge: Judson Press, 1975.

10

Spiritual Gifts for Elders and Deacons

Purpose of the Lesson

This lesson is designed to show the relationship of Spirit-given abilities to the various ministries of the Church. There is a tendency to substitute natural talents for spiritual gifts. Both should be consecrated to God and used for His glory, but for effectiveness in ministry the gifts of the Holy Spirit must be given priority.

Questions for Discussion

1. What is a spiritual gift?
2. How do spiritual gifts differ from natural talents?
3. What does the principle of spiritual gifts teach regarding the structure of the local church?
4. If one is gifted in an area of ministry, is study and preparation for that ministry necessary? Why or why not?
5. When do believers receive spiritual gifts?
6. What is the relationship between one's place in the body of Christ and one's spiritual gifts?
7. Do you think that God may add gifts in the course of our Christian life to meet the needs of expanding responsibilities? Why or why not?

8. What is the relationship between spiritual qualifications, natural qualifications and spiritual gifts?
9. Do leaders need to be able to identify their gifts in order to take up the work of elders or deacons? Is the call of the brethren sometimes an indication that others recognize our gifts even when we do not?
10. Are spiritual gifts as necessary to those who handle the financial and management responsibilities as they are to those who minister exclusively in spiritual matters?

The Teaching Plan

The impact of this lesson can be increased by a visual presentation of the gifts. Prepare in advance a composite list of the gifts using First Corinthians 12:8-10, 28-31; Romans 12:6-18, Ephesians 4:11. Guide the class through the exercise of grouping the gifts in categories. The following may be considered:

1. Administration

2. Service

3. Proclamation

4. Demonstration of God's power

5. Training and edification

Go through this list a second time and relate the office of the pastor, lay-elders, deacons and other church leaders to the gifts. Be careful to point out that every member of the body has a gift that should be used for the building up of the church. Does the lack of competent leadership in local churches relate to the neglect of gifts? Can we grieve the Holy Spirit by failing to use our gifts for the good of the body of Christ? Is there a relationship between the Spirit-filled life and the exercise of gifts? How important is obedience to the proper use of gifts? Would the intelligent relating of gifts to concrete ministries reduce some of the fantasy relating to gifts in today's church? Explain.

Resource Material

Bridges, Donald and Phypers, David. *Spiritual Gifts and the Church.* Downers Grove: InterVarsity Press, 1971.

Brow, Robert. *The Church.* Grand Rapids: William B. Eerdman, 1968.

Flynn, Leslie B. *19 Gifts of the Spirit.* Harrisburg: Christian Publications, Inc., 1974.

11

The Preparation of Elders and Deacons

Purpose of the Lesson

The structured training course for the lay-elders and deacons serves only as the threshold to a continuing experience of learning and personal development. The thrust of this lesson is to inspire the elected church officers to self-improvement spiritually and mentally. Suggestions are made as to basic areas where ongoing training is essential if the elder or deacon is to grow with his job.

Questions for Discussion

1. Since a layman has only a limited amount of time for ministry, what ground rules should he use in selecting priorities?
2. Name some situations in which the lay-elder or deacon may need to choose between other good activities and the demands of his calling as elder or deacon.
3. How does one get back into study when he has not been doing it for a number of years? Is this a spiritual discipline?

4. Make a list of reasons why a church leader should have good Bible knowledge.
5. How could the call to serve as an elder or deacon affect your family? Is it fair to ask your family to make sacrifices for the sake of ministry?
6. What importance do you place upon the leader's knowledge of doctrine?
7. Why should he know the distinctives of your denomination?
8. How would you rate reading as a practice necessary to personal growth? (Check a concordance for references to reading.)
9. What can an elder or deacon do to learn more about people? Why is this essential to his ministry?
10. Why is continuous training in leadership skills so important to a church officer?

The Teaching Plan

The elder or deacon who has not studied for years will need some convincing evidence that he should begin such a program for himself as this lesson proposes. The Scriptures will be the most persuasive means of convincing him that he should study. The first segment of the class should be devoted to a study of the following passages which deal with the importance of discipline in the life of a Christian worker: First Timothy 4:6-16; Second Timothy 2:14-15; 3:14-17; Titus 2:1-10. These passages urge those who minister to study and read so they may know sound doctrine. Their teaching can only have integrity if they have given themselves to the hard work of learning the Scriptures well. The ministry of the Holy Spirit should be emphasized at this point. The work of study can be turned into the joy of learning under the guidance of the Spirit. Men called of God to serve the body of Christ have every reason to expect the help of the Holy Spirit in preparation for service.

The kind of self-study this lesson calls for is not just a series of studies but a lifestyle. Time is set aside each day for reading good books and for Bible study. Those who are facing this obligation for the first time will need assurance that the day-by-day building up of their knowledge of Scripture will pay rich dividends.

The church should provide for continuous training beyond the personal program of self-improvement each elder and deacon may develop. At least two courses a year should be offered by the pastor or trained lay leader. The class may want to discuss the kind of lay training program the church should provide. Some class time can be devoted to the kinds of books each elder and deacon should read. Provide the class with a bibliography of books available in the church library and from the denomination's publishing house.

Resource Material

Eims, Leroy. *Be the Leader You Were Meant to Be.* Wheaton: Victor Books, 1977.

Engstrom, Ted W. *The Making of a Christian Leader.* Grand Rapids: Zondervan Publishing House, 1977.

Gangel, Kenneth O. *So You Want to Be a Leader.* Harrisburg: Christian Publications, Inc., 1973.

Elders and Deacons and the Denomination

Purpose of the Lesson

Church officers need an understanding of the larger church body to which their congregation belongs. The purpose of this lesson is to give the elders and deacons an overview of The Christian and Missionary Alliance and to show how the local church relates to each level of the denominational structure. Since these officers must at times relate to district and national programs, they should have some knowledge of both levels of administration. They may also have opportunities for service on these levels. The better informed the local church leadership is regarding the district, national and international work of the denomination, the better their support of the church's worldwide ministry. This lesson provides an ideal opportunity for discussing not only the government of the church but the programs of the church both at home and overseas.

If time permits a brief summary of the historical roots of the denomination would be helpful. Especially important in this lesson is an emphasis on the kind and philosophy of church government in The Christian and Missionary Alliance. The final authority of the denomination is the legislative assembly. This pattern is consistent at every level from the local church to the national level. The legislative action of General Council and the district conferences is mandatory. Respect for constituted authority is basic in the Alliance form of government. The various constitutions for the local church, the district and the national level provide for delegated authority to be used by the executive committee between meetings of the full assembly. The quality of service rendered by the church's elected officers can be greatly improved by their understanding and supporting these principles.

Questions for Discussion

1. What does the word *denomination* mean? What is the essential difference between sectarianism and denominationalism?
2. What are the benefits and services the denomination gives to the local churches?
3. Discuss the provisions made for lay involvement in the district and at the national level of the denomination.
4. How does the local church's government fit into the government of the district and of the General Council?
5. Why is lay involvement important in the church's legislative assemblies?
6. How does lay involvement with parachurch groups and transdenominationial groups compare with involvement in one's own denomination?
7. What are some of the doors of ministry that can be opened for elders and deacons in the work of the district?
8. In what specific ways will the local church be helped by district activity?
9. Discuss the important relationship between the constitutional requirements placed on local churches and

the objectives of ministry The Christian and Missionary Alliance seeks to carry out.

10. What direct benefits come to a local church as a result of its involvement in the world missionary outreach of the larger fellowship?

The Teaching Plan

Each member of the class should be given a copy of The Manual of the Christian and Missionary Alliance well in advance of this class. Give some reading assignments to the entire class and then ask some class members to give an oral report on their reading. One person should be assigned to read all the legislation regarding General Council and report to the class. The leader can point out the significant fact that lay involvement could be doubled and still not meet the level suggested by the constitution. The leader or someone acquainted with General Council may be asked to share with the class what takes place at a General Council meeting. A similar process could be followed in informing the class about the district conference. If the district superintendent were nearby he could be invited to address the class concerning the ministry of the district. The relationship of each part of the church to the whole can be demonstrated by use of overhead projection provided for this lesson. If you do not have an overhead projector available, reproduce the charts on a chalkboard.

Resource Material

Current Manual of The Christian and Missionary Alliance District By-laws.

Hunter, J.H. *Beside All Waters*. Harrisburg: Christian Publications, Inc.,1964.

Stoesz, Samuel. *Understanding My Church*. Harrisburg: Christian Publications, Inc., 1983.

13

The Election and Consecration of Elders and Deacons

Purpose of the Lesson

This lesson stresses the need for understanding the process by which the church selects its officers. The fundamentals of this important procedure can be found in the New Testament. There are enough examples from the practice of the early church to know that they considered the election of elders and deacons very important. The Scriptures without exception indicate that elected officers were publicly commissioned to do their work.

Questions for Discussion

1. What are some of the reasons for the church's apathy toward its annual business meeting?
2. How would you defend from the Scriptures the integrity of such a meeting?
3. What should be the place of prayer in the church's preparation for the business meeting?
4. What can the nominating committee do to screen the possible candidates for the offices of elder and deacon? Should they have their Bibles open to First Timothy chapter 3 and Titus?

5. What could your local church do to improve the annual business meeting?
6. What kinds of sermons would help guide the congregation in their responsibilities? Do many members really understand their obligation?
7. Do you think the elective process is better than the ecclesiastical appointment of officers? Why or why not?
8. What are some of the pitfalls of the elective process?
9. What is ordination? Why are pastors ordained?
10. Why are lay-elders and deacons commissioned by the laying on of hands?

The Teaching Plan

The nature of this lesson provides an excellent opportunity to discuss with the lay-elders and deacons what the local church constitution says about the electoral process. Copies of your denomination's manual and the local church by-laws should be available to the class. Use the blackboard or an overhead projector to compare the procedure in the constitution with the biblical practices. While the nomenclature may be different, the principles are the same.

The heart of this lesson is to instill a high regard for the place of the church fellowship in selecting its leaders. How does the Holy Spirit use this process? How would you account for the poor judgments sometimes made by the church? How can the church election be safeguarded?

The closing section of the chapter deals with the commissioning of the lay-elders and deacons. This may be a new concept to many in the class. They may be confused as to how this ceremony relates to ordination which most denominations practice only for pastors. A brief study on the nature and meaning of ordination would be helpful. Point out to the class that the difference between pastoral ordination and commissioning of lay-elders and deacons is a matter of degrees and of function. The laying on of hands to commission lay-elders and deacons symbolizes the church's recognition of their being set apart to those ministries. The church's understanding of the ordination of pastors has enlarged across the years to imply an act of consecration, a special enduement of the Holy Spirit, a certification of the church's concurrence that the ordained is truly called of God to the gospel ministry.

Resource Material

Current Manual of The Christian and Missionary Alliance.

Robert, Henry M. *Robert's Rules of Order.* "Ordination and Commissioning." Spire Books. Old Tappan: Fleming H. Revell.

Appendix A

An Historical Review of Eldership Since the Reformation

The reformers not only sought to restore apostolic doctrine in the message of the Church but they sought to restore apostolic practice in the order of the Church. Zwingli, Knox and Calvin taught their followers that the apostolic order recognized pastor, elders and deacons for each local assembly. The pastor was the chief minister of the congregation. While the pastor was an ordained elder, the church also set apart lay-elders and deacons to act as supportive leaders. The pastor is called a teaching elder and the lay-elders are known as ruling elders. This concept has survived under the name Presbyterianism.

The Episcopal tradition reflecting the Catholic system made the bishop a separate office from the elder and designated the bishop, elder and deacon as clergy! Lay leadership was developed under other titles.

The Baptist tradition maintains that pastors only are elders. The functions assigned by other communions to lay-elders and deacons are delegated by Baptists entirely to the deacons.

When the Lutheran reformation became a state church a grass roots movement called the Anabaptists began in

Germany, Switzerland and the low countries. They were given this name because they re-baptized their converts from Lutheranism.

Among the Anabaptists a plurality of elders became the pattern for local church leadership. Except in some of the fringe groups of Anabaptists, recognition was given to a presiding elder in the assembly. One of the elders was elevated to be the leader of the group. His function resembled the president of the Jewish synagogue and many of the primitive Christian assemblies. Anabaptists recognized the principle of one in charge from among a plurality of elders. This system differs little from the Presbyterian format.

In the mid-1800s a movement began in England under the leadership of J.N. Darby. Darby and his associates were concerned with a recovery of New Testament church order. They were persuaded that a plurality of elders was the only pattern of church government the Scriptures allowed. The pastoral function, according to their teaching, was distributed among all the elders. Based on their view of the headship of Christ, the Brethren concluded that the local church not have a pastor/leader, but leadership was shared within the eldership. The movement took an anti-clergy viewpoint.

Recent church renewal literature has reflected the Darby position. Unfortunately, too many renewal writers have failed to see that the experience of the Church since the Reformation has produced two distinct views of the plurality of elders. It should be remembered that the followers of Darby were breaking out of Episcopalianism and tended to overreact. The peculiarities of their ecclesiology also affected their conception of the role of the elder. They see the local church as the only visibility of the Church of Christ here on earth. The government of the local assembly in Darby's teaching rests entirely on charismatic leadership as distinguished from office-bearing leadership.

To argue that the abuses of power by the clergy discredit the concept of office in the church is hardly credible. Godly, dedicated, sacrificial leadership is the norm in both the Old Testament and the New Testament. The deviation from that kind of true ministry does not necessarily disprove the effectiveness of the system. The defect was often in the character of the leader and not in the system.

Appendix B

Job Description for Elders

Qualifications:

1. Born-again, "full of faith and the Holy Ghost," of good reputation among those within and without the church, the husband of one wife who rules well his own house.
2. Experienced in the Word of God and prayer, so as to scripturally aid those under their watch care.
3. Have spiritual sensitivity and ability to minister in comfort, exhortation and discipline.
4. Have a willing spirit to go as the representative of the Lord Jesus when assigned, being loyal to the doctrines and constitution of our church.
5. Hospitable, a generous giver and faithful in church attendance.

Responsibilities:

1. Assist the pastor in the spiritual work of the church.
2. Constitute the committee on church membership.
3. Constitute the committee on all matters of church disciplines (See church by-laws, section on membership—discipline.)

4. May serve as a communion steward in administering the Lord's Supper.
5. Assist candidates at baptismal services.
6. Pray and anoint the sick when called.
7. Annually review the membership and bring it up to date.
8. Visit members and adherents, especially the discouraged, the troubled, the oppressed and the weaker brethren. As feasible, elders may be responsible for a given number of church families, whom they shall visit at least annually.
9. Meet with the chairman of the elders for prayer fifteen minutes before services.
10. Report in writing quarterly to the executive committee and annually to the congregation.
11. Be responsible for special ministries as assigned by the pastor.

From *The Church Handbook* of First Alliance Church, New York City, N.Y. Used by permission.

Appendix C

Job Description for Deacons

Qualifications:

1. Spiritually sound and pure, having a good reputation for leadership in both their community and home.
2. The husband of one wife who is similarly qualified, having his house in subjection.
3. Able to assume delegated responsibilities and report to those in authority over him.
4. Gladhearted men whom the Scriptures say have chosen a good office which is manifested by their loyalty to the Lord and our church's doctrines and constitution.
5. Hospitable, liberal in giving and faithful in attendance at church services.
6. The above qualifications are to be considered amplifications of those set forth in the constitution.

Responsibilities:

1. Maintain the church's parsonages and buildings, including the care of lawns and landscaping.
2. Provide security for all church attendants and for building lock-up.
3. Supervise the parking facilities.
4. Serve as the welcoming committee.

5. Meet regularly or upon call of the chairman to conduct business.
6. Give a progress report to the executive committee quarterly through the chairman and to the congregation annually.
7. Additional responsibilities may be assigned by the executive committee or by the congregation.
8. With the deaconesses promote fellowship to members and visitors.
9. With the deaconesses may share responsibility for distributing benevolences.

From *The Church Handbook* of First Alliance Church, New York City, N.Y. Used by permission.

Appendix D

Job Descriptions for Deaconesses

Qualifications:

1. Ladies of high spiritual caliber and members in good standing of the church.
2. Friendly, empathetic, interested in the needs of others and able to take group responsibilities.
3. Live in the biblical pattern of modest dress and conduct.
4. Have a keen sense of loyalty and dedication to the Lord Jesus and to His Church and its teachings and constitution.

Responsibilities

1. Meet regularly for prayer and business. Their business shall be conducted through telephone captains between meetings.
2. Arrange for the communion services, including ordering supplies, care of linens and preparation of elements and cleanup.
3. With the Home Department visit the sick, the infirm and the bereaved. Send cards when appropriate to encourage and comfort. It is suggested that deacon-

esses include Scripture reading and prayer in their visits.

4. Assist families in bereavement with food service or personal help as needed.
5. Assist baptismal candidates with robes and other helping ministries.
6. Evaluate reports of special need and distribute benevolences.
7. With the deacons make a special effort to welcome visitors and new members.
8. Arrange for the sanctuary flowers to be taken to a hospital patient or to a shut-in.
9. Plan special activities for our retired and elderly members, in addition to the regular services.
10. Arrange hospitality for visiting pastors, evangelists and missionaries.
11. Appoint and supervise the kitchen committee.
12. Provide counseling for women and girls when needed.

From *The Church Handbook* of First Alliance Church, New York City, N.Y. Used by permission.

Appendix E

Ordination

The first and most important justification for the church practice of ordination is biblical. In both the Old Testament and the New Testament the office bearers of the household of faith were ordained. The practice of ordination was not invented by the church in her subsequent history, but had its origin in the inspired action of the Savior and His apostles.

Christ ordained twelve apostles from among His disciples and trained them to be the foundational ministers of His church. The apostles as a matter of course ordained elders wherever churches were planted. Some brief glimpses of the ordination ritual in the apostolic church have been preserved in the Scriptures. It was usually attended with fasting, prayer and the laying on of hands. Spiritual gifts were sometimes imparted on the occasion or ordination.

The words used in the original language for ordination can be translated "appoint," or "to put in place," to install in an office. Ordination is, then, that process by which the church selects, appoints and places in office its ministers. Ordination does not make the candidate a minister. He must have received a distinct call from God and an anointing from the Holy Spirit for the ministry to which he is called. The divine order for God's house requires the confirmation of that call by the church. The process and ceremony of ordination attests the call, the preparation and the spiritual fitness of the man seeking to enter the ministry.

Commissioning Local Church Officers

The lay ministry of elders and deacons, like the pastoral ministry, requires a call from God and a willingness to prepare for the ministry these two offices afford.

The church selects the elders and deacons by the process of congregational election. They set them apart for this work by the laying on of hands. By this action the church confirms and commissions its elders and deacons. The faithful observance of this practice will serve to impress the congregation with both the seriousness and the sacredness of the offices of lay elders and deacons.

While ordination and commissioning are not identical, they are related. They differ in degree and in function. They are similar in that by each ceremony the church sends forth her appointed servants to their work. The experience of the church has made ordination to the gospel ministry a significant step in the life of the man of God. He spends years preparing for it. His fellow ministers examine his call to preach, his personal and devotional life and his doctrinal position. The ordination of ministers is the prerogative of the district. A special committee of experienced pastors are elected to oversee this work. For at least two years the candidate for ordination attends in-service training meetings, reads a select bibliography of books and is counseled by a senior minister in preparation for ordination.